BAUCHER AND HIS SCHOOL

GENERAL Albert-Eugène Edouard DECARPENTRY

With **Appendix I: Recollections**
From **LOUIS RUL** *and* **EUGÈNE CARON**

With **Appendix II: Commentary by LOUIS SEEGER**
From his pamphlet:
MR. BAUCHER AND HIS ART:
A SERIOUS WORD WITH THE RIDERS OF GERMANY

Translation by **Michael L. M. Fletcher**
Edited by **Richard and Frances Williams**

Copyright © 2011 by Xenophon Press LLC

Translated by Michael L. M. Fletcher

Edited by Richard and Frances Williams

All rights reserved. No part of this work may be reproduced or transmitted in any form or by any means, electronic or mechanical, including photocopying, or by any information storage or retrieval system except by a written permission from the publisher.

Published by Xenophon Press LLC

7518 Bayside Road, Franktown, Virginia 23354-2106, U.S.A.

Xenophonpress@gmail.com

www.xenophonpress.com

| ISBN-10 | 0933316208 |
| ISBN-13 | 9780933316201 |

Front cover image: Baucher riding Buridan in piaffe.

GENERAL DECARPENTRY

BAUCHER AND HIS SCHOOL

*Portrait of Baucher
by Giraud*

Translated by Michael L. M. Fletcher
Edited by Richard and Frances Williams

TABLE OF CONTENTS

Foreword to the English Translation iii
Dedication by the Publisher v
Introduction to the English Edition vii
Glossary xi
Author's Foreword 1
Author's Dedication 6
Chapter I – The Early Years 7
Chapter II – The Circus 11
Chapter III – Baucher, The Man, the Écuyer, the Writer 31
Chapter IV – The Principle of the Method 39
Chapter V – The Procedures 45
Chapter VI – The Results 55
Chapter VII – Experiment with the Method in the Army 77
Chapter VIII – In the Capitals of Europe 99
Chapter IX – The Second Manner 105
Chapter X – The Last Years 111
Chapter XI – Baucher's School 115
Chapter XII – And now? 129
Appendix I – Recollections from Rul and Caron 133
Appendix II – Louis Seeger's Pamphlet 173
Bibliography 205
Credits 205
Xenophon Press Library 207

TABLE OF ILLUSTRATIONS

Portrait of Baucher (by Giraud) .... Title Page

Baucher on Partisan 21

Baucher on Capitaine at the Pirouette 26

Origins of the École de Cavalerie 30

Caricature of Baucher by Lorentz: The Écuyer 38

Monsieur Nestier riding Florido 44

Caricature of Baucher by Lorentz: The Writer 54

Baucher on Partisan: Piaffe 64

The Experiment in Paris 84

Baucher riding Capitaine 132

FOREWORD TO THE ENGLISH TRANSLATION

It is with great pleasure that I am writing the forward for Michael Fletcher's translation of *Baucher et son École* by Decarpentry. It is with profound sadness to all of us that the passing of Michael will prevent him from seeing the result of his hard, difficult and very well-done work.

This book is important to all serious riders interested in studying the history of equitation and the influence of Baucher on today's riding. François Baucher was very controversial during his entire life and in his written works. He continually made changes according to his new experiences and studies. This constant evolution is paralleled in this book. His techniques have, in some cases, changed very drastically, but the principles remained the same, clearly explained in this treatise. The historical part of Baucher's life and the important influence on equitation are both presented, not only with respect to military equitation but also, more importantly, the influence of equitation on the intellectual and artistic world of the time.

Once again, thank you, Michael, and Richard Williams and Xenophon Press for making available to English speaking riders such an enlightening, entertaining, and educational translation.

Major Miguel Tavora, (Portuguese Cavalry Retired)

DEDICATION BY THE PUBLISHER

This translation project belonged to Michael L. M. Fletcher, a dedicated equestrian with a passion for bringing important French works to English speaking dressage enthusiasts. Michael's tireless work produced this faithful, first ever, complete translation of *Baucher et son École*, by General Decarpentry. We dedicate this great work to Michael. He was not able to see it in print due to his untimely passing. Michael L. M. Fletcher's carefully prepared glossary is provided as an aid too the translation of French terms used throughout the text.

Major Tavora was instrumental in assisting with fine tuning the translation. Ivan Bezugloff provided inspiration as the founder of Xenophon Press. We are continuing his mission of bringing important equestrian works to print in the English language lest they be lost in obscurity or remain appreciated only by readers of the original language.

Frances and Richard Williams, Xenophon Press

INTRODUCTION
TO THE ENGLISH TRANSLATION

Albert Decarpentry, known best for his work: *Academic Equitation*, was a prolific author of six known equestrian texts. His expertise with François Baucher's teachings came from having relatives and mentors who were direct students of the master. Decarpentry presents a detailed and sympathetic biography of this pivotal figure in the history of equitation. Decarpentry chose to include Louis Seeger's pamphlet, *A Serious Word with the Riders of Germany*, attacking Baucher. It is because Decarpentry incorporated this negative account of Baucher, that we have, in turn, included it in the English translation.

It is important to recognize that Seeger's pamphlet was written in 1853 in response to Baucher's well publicized First Method. Baucher was an experimenter, and innovator, constantly modifying his method and techniques. Baucher's theories were published frequently. Often those in print at any given time were not consistent with his current practices. Seeger was reacting to an immature Baucherist philosophy and method. Seeger was responding to the information and presentations that he had at the time. He was also exceedingly proud and was working diligently to put forth his own definitive method in his *System der Reitkunst*, 1844. The closing of the aristocratic court riding School of Versailles in 1830 coincided with the forced abdication of Charles X. The Bourbons were out of favor and with the disbursement of the faculty, the main support of horsemanship shifted to the nationalistic military academies and the circus, favored by the rising bourgeois class. François Baucher, a commoner, rejected the old, aristocratic system and tried to replace it with his own, revolutionary, new ideas.

The lasting effect of the French Revolution was the significant political shift championing the common man. Baucher and his followers were sympathizers with the Napoleonic regime. Germany still resented Napoleon's attack and occupation. Seeger championed the methods of de la Guérinière in words, if not in actual practice. Seeger trained horses for the circus, as did Baucher. Seeger likely felt threatened by his competitor, Baucher, who produced astonishing results in a much shorter time than traditional horsemanship, so he tried to discredit him.

The following quote from Dom Diogo de Bragança's *Dressage in the French Tradition*, (Xenophon Press 2011) eloquently presents the struggle between French and German dressage -- a preoccupation in the equestrian world starting in the nineteenth century with the rise of German and French nationalism.

> *It has been noted, about the characteristics of the dressage tests of today, that exactitude – the primary occupation of the German School – has been preferred to beauty, that has been the primary preoccupation of the French School, even if that beauty was not accompanied by a perfect precision in the obedience to the aids. The question goes back a long way, and great riders have compared the German and French Schools, ever since Baucherism provoked a schism from the old school doctrine that had been followed unanimously and without great differences of interpretation by all of the European equestrian academies.*
>
> *The German School, which has always applied the teaching of the Old French School with a view to obtaining great precision in the movements, was in open war with the Baucherism that was presenting a new method to explore every horse's possibilities. The Old School in France accorded great value to brilliance in equestrian art. Baucher's techniques, which produced even more brilliance, delivered a severe blow to the Old School. And while France boasted of having one more great écuyer, it was mainly Germany that took to heart the defense of the old manner.*
>
> *Witness the pamphlet published by the German Louis Seeger in Berlin, in 1853. His "Sérieux Avertissement aux Cavaliers*

d'Allemagne" (Serious Warning to Riders of Germany), French translation, excerpts in Appendix to Decarpentry, "Baucher et son École", Paris, 1987)(Appendix II to Decarpentry, "François Baucher and His School", Xenophon Press 2011) put German riders on guard against the propaganda of Baucher's method. Seeger sought to reduce the value of Baucherism to nothing by contrasting it to the advantages of the old method.

One cannot say that Seeger supported his critique on very plausible arguments, even though in the middle of the XIX century, he was one of the most renowned German écuyers.

For reasons not well known, Baucher's presentations in Berlin were made on very mediocre horses. But in justification, 'Blacknick' or 'Rufus' which could not have had the elegance and brilliance of a fine horse, proved that their lack of blood and their defective conformation did not impede them from executing the most difficult airs.

Seeger's criticism dates from 1853. Baucherism, at that time, had not attained the maturity that would lead it to the Second Manner. Seeger, concerned with showing that his method was the better of the two, described himself as the successor to La Guérinière. However, he applied those techniques with his Germanic temperament, and thus greatly modified the horsemanship that he claimed to represent.

The technical criticisms of Baucher that Seeger addressed:

Horizontal balance (as practiced by Baucher) can only serve for everyday riding, not for Haute École.

Baucher's rassembler required the horse to bring his four legs together, which often put him on his shoulders instead of making him flex from the haunches to the stifles.

The trot is heavy, and in piaffe, the hind legs escape laterally instead of advancing under the body, while the forelegs do not lift sufficiently.

At the canter, the horse carries himself alternately on the forehand and on the hindquarters "in a movement that presents a certain analogy to that of a wave."

Finally after even many more criticisms, Seeger finished by treating Baucher as a charlatan, and called him the "grave digger of French dressage."

".... let us make the point using what General Decarpentry said on the same subject, at the beginning of his Équitation Academique" (1949).

"When the School of Horsemanship at Versailles, heir to the academies of the Renaissance, finally closed its doors for good in 1830, its teaching was supposed to be passed on at the School at Saumur. But when Comte d'Aure, though a student at the famous Academy, was named Écuyer en chef at Saumur, he put academic dressage to the side, and made a more practical method prevail. His method was, in his view, more suitable for a military school. This did not prevent him, as well as the écuyers that were under his orders, from practicing, individually and also in reprises (organized group presentations,) the School airs and jumps inspired by those of the School of Versailles."

"The appearance of Baucherism started a new era in dressage."

Aware of Baucher's contemporary critics, Decarpentry presents both sides of the Baucher opinion sets in the spirit of full disclosure. It is thanks to Decarpentry's work, *François Baucher and his School,* that we are able to make a fair evaluation of the impact of Baucher on the history of horsemanship. Innovations introduced by Baucher have been adopted at the highest levels of international competition. While one man could not pretend to match the collective knowledge of centuries of equestrian practice and culture, Baucher experimented, discovered, innovated, and left a lasting impact on the course of equestrian history and practice.

Richard Williams, Xenophon Press

GLOSSARY

Académie d'Équitation de L'Europe:
  European Academy of Equitation

Administration des Haras:
  National office for the supervision of studs

Amazone:
  Female rider, usually side-saddle

Anciens:
  old masters, old écuyers, also army veterans and old soldiers

appréciation:
  assessment, estimation, valuation, perception, appreciation

à contre-poil:
  against the hair (coat), the wrong way

à-propos:
  just in time, with the right timing and measure

attitude d'ensemble:
  attitude or position of the whole, the horse's frame and top line

Auguste:
  ancestor of the Red Clown

au temps:
  a tempi, at every time, beat, every stride

baladin:
  wandering minstrel

balancé:
  the forehand stepping one step side to side making the shoulders swing from side to side, particularly in the piaffe

balancer latéralment, se:
  the hindquarters stepping one step side to side making the croup swing from side to side

Bauchérisant:
> loosely: Baucherising, Baucheriser, one who Baucherises, making Baucherist changes to d'Aurist or even traditional equitation

Bauchérisme:
> Baucherism, advocating the training, or the training itself, of horses in the Baucher Manner

Bauchérist:
> one who practices or supports Baucherism

bois:
> woods

bouton:
> usually button, but here used to mean the sliding keeper used to adjust the length of un-held curb reins

cabrade:
> a rear

Carabiniers:
> a heavy cavalry tracing its history to mounted police

Carbonari:
> secret anti-monarchist movement originating in Italy

Carré Marigny:
> Marigny Square

Cent Gardes:
> One Hundred Guards, personal horse guards for Emperor Napoleon III

c'est si beau:
> it's so beautiful, good, great

chasseurs:
> hunters, a type of light cavalry, distinctly French but similar to Hussars

chasser le devant:
> chase the forehand

chef d'escadron:
> Squadron Chief, usually a Captain commanding one squadron of cavalry

Chef d'escadrons:
> Chief of Squadrons, equivalent to Major or Commandant, but commanding more than one squadron

Commandant:
> usually a major commanding an entity but in the case of the Cavalry School, a general

communards:
>early communists, Paris, 1871

Comte:
>Count

Corps:
>used here in a general sense of "body" rather than a formal designation such as a Corps as a group of usually three Divisions and part of an Army in the field, or as in the Cavalry Corps as part of the entire Army

Courbette:
>from a levade or a pesade, the horse jumps forward on his hind legs one or more times remaining upright

cuirassiers:
>heavier cavalry that wore breastplates

débats:
>debates

dégingandé:
>one who, in his movements and in his attitude, appears to have something out of order, lanky, ungainly, gangling

des cavaliers anciens et vigoureux:
>experienced and vigorous riders, with a subtext of old soldiers

doublé:
>ninety degree turn off the track to the centre, then, optionally, across to the opposite track, ninety degree turn in the same direction or optionally turn in the opposite direction for change of hand

doubler:
>The infinitive form of doublé and meaning the same thing; the more normal usage and pronounced the same way

dragons:
>dragoons, light cavalry derived from mounted infantry

Duc:
>Duke

École:
>School

École de Cavalerie:
>Cavalry School

École de Dressage et d'Équitation:
>School of Dressage and Equitation

École d'État-Major:
    Headquarters School

École d'instruction des troupes à cheval:
    School of instruction for mounted troops

École National d'Équitation:
    National School of Equitation

Écuries:
    Stables

Écurie, la Grande:
    The Large Stable, generally devoted to saddle horses

Écurie, la Petite:
    The Small Stable, generally devoted to harness horses

Écuyer:
    Trainer-rider, usually a teacher

Écuyères:
    Female riders, usually in the circus, often credited with training that they sometimes left to their instructors

Écuyer en chef:
    Chief trainer-rider-teacher

effet d'ensemble:
    Effect of the whole, coordinated effect

Élève:
    Student

E semper (Latin):
    And always

faire de phrases:
    Idiomatic expression meaning in this case: without lecturing

faire le nique:
    Loosely: thumb the nose

Faubourg:
    Suburban neighborhood

fils du peuple:
    Son of the people

fin prêt:
    Ready to go

gambades:
    Leaping capers, gambols

Garde Consulaire:
  Consul's Guard

Garde Municipale:
  Municipal Guard (of Paris)

Garde Nationale:
  National Guard, a militia based in Paris

gens du monde:
  People of the world, worldly people, society

Gradés:
  Officers and Non-Commissioned Officers

Guides:
  Cavalry assigned to the protection of an Army or Corps Headquarters and the Commanding officer

Haute École:
  High School

Héros de Juillet:
  Heros of July, see Trois Glorieuses

individus louches:
  Shady characters

in petto (Latin):
  In secret

jambes plaquées:
  Legs plastered (or jammed) on to the horse

jambette:
  The lifting of a single foreleg as when a horse is pawing, then the extension of that leg, and ultimately on command, holding the leg in extension. A step of the Spanish walk

lançade:
  The horse lunges up and forward

lapsus:
  Slip of the tongue, pen

Lèse-équitation:
  Insult to equitation

levade:
  The horse raises his forehand with his truck at an angle of 30 – 35o and remains there for a few moments

lieues:
  leagues, approximately 4 kilometers, depending on era and usage

maître:
: master trainer-teacher-rider

manège:
: riding school, hall, arena, usually indoor

Manège des Pages:
: riding school ostensibly for the court pages, but functioned as a cadet corps for the cavalry

maréchal:
: marshall, commanding officer of an army

Maréchal de Camp:
: Brigadier (General)

Maréchal des Logis:
: non-commissioned officer rank in the French cavalry roughly equivalent to Quartermaster from Sergeant to Warrant Officer

Maître:
: Riding Master

masses individuelles:
: individual clothing and equipment account

mauvais cœur:
: bad heart, spirit, disposition

méchant:
: malicious, nasty

mézair:
: a movement comprising a series of levades with small jumps between

mise en main:
: put in hand, the *ramener* along with the relaxation of the jaw, often inaccurately translated as: put on the bit. Note that Seeger did not seek relaxation of the jaw and his *mise en main* is closer to putting on the bit

mouvement de harper:
: veterinary term, also used in English, meaning raising the limbs without bending, associated rocking movement of the hindquarters

Note de Service:
: an order, which may lay down a policy or procedure, expressed in a letter or memorandum

novum organum (Latin):
: new instrument, taken from the title of a philosophical work by Francis Bacon

plaquées:
> jammed or gripped (against the horse)

parade:
> see parade-éclair. Not so dramatically quick

parade-éclair:
> lightening stop. Halt from gallop or canter, or extended or lengthened trot

pas compté, à:
> at a counted walk, cadenced walk

pas de deux:
> dance or freestyle for two

pas de quatre:
> dance or freestyle for four

perruques:
> periwigs, a wig, especially one worn by men in the 17th and 18th centuries

Pesade:
> the horse raises the forehand balancing on his hind legs with the trunk at a 450 angle and remains there for a few moments

petit trot:
> small trot, anything from a jog to a highly collected trot. A lengthened trot was called "grand trot" while the rising trot, "trot enlevé" was not yet in use

pianotage:
> as in playing the piano on the reins

pianoter:
> see *pianotage*. Baucher riding with the left hand would use the fingers of his right to create pressure on one or another rein

piquer:
> hunt rider, so named from the days when they hunted with spears

piste:
> track, the outside track of the circus ring, circus ring

placer:
> make the horse take a balance or position, also in a sense, restrict a bend or flexion of the poll. Making the horse round from behind while in the *ramener* and usually in a *pli*

pli:
> the slightly bent (flexed, lateral positioning) of the horse while travelling on a straight single track

plié:
    to bend

pointer:
    to rear, with one or both forelegs reaching out forward

porte-manteau, en:
    carrying his coat, stuck out

qui se rassemble:
    one which rassemblers himself, which collects himself

ramener:
    horse's head position with the neck arched and the forehead at the vertical

ramener outré:
    exaggerated ramener; the horse's nose approaches the chest

rassemblé:
    in the rassembler, collected

rassembler:
    collection of the horse, reducing his base of support in place, as well as on the move, exemplified in the *piaffe*

redopp:
    variation on *terre-à-terre*

relèvement:
    the training procedure of raising the head and neck

ressorts:
    springs, resources, joints

rétif:
    rebellious, stubborn

rue:
    street

Saint-Cyr:
    The Officer Candidate School

salto mortale:
    somersault of death

sans-culottes:
    without breeches, a term applied to radical working class movements. By 1848, the term was no longer used in France, but was used as an insult by the aristocrats outside of France

Service de la Place:
    The guarding, patrolling, defense, and, in some cases, policing of a position, fortification, or garrison: in this case, Paris

sou:
: coin, one tenth of a franc, sometimes referred to as centime

Sous-écuyer:
: assistant écuyer, under rider

Sous-Lieutenant:
: Second or Sub-Lieutenant

Sous-Mâitres:
: Non-commissioned riding masters

Sous-Officiers:
: Non-Commissioned Officers

terre-à-terre:
: a type of very collected canter in two time, usually a preparation for school jumps

tirez-dessus – tapez-dedans:
: push and pull

trainer le derrière:
: drag the hindquarters

tride:
: lively, quick, short and ready

Trois Glorieuses:
: The "three glorious days," the three-day Revolution of July 27, 28 and 29 in 1830 in Paris of popular uprising after which Charles X was forced to leave the throne to his cousin, the Duke of Orleans, future Louis-Philippe

trot marché:
: a diagonalized walk approaching a trot

truquer:
: to fix, with the connotation of rigging or a trick

Ultras:
: a name applied to the Royalists of the time

vélites:
: Skirmishers

Vicomte:
: Viscount

AUTHOR'S FOREWORD

There are few riders, even amongst those who ride only on Sunday, that do not at least recognize the name BAUCHER, the greatest *écuyer* of all time.

On the other hand, there are fewer still that know any more than that about this Master of Equestrian Art.

Perhaps my fellow members of the Order of Saint George might take an interest in reading these pages consecrated to the memory of Baucher and the story of his method that just about one hundred years ago (from 1948) definitely seemed destined to replace all that experience and tradition had left us in the precepts for the training and riding of the saddle horse.

From 340 B.C., when Xenophon wrote the first treatise on equitation that would come down to us, until 1842, when Baucher published his new method, riders of all countries had used nearly identical procedures to educate and direct their horses.

Discovered by empiricism, perfected over the course of more than a millennium of experience, adapted to particular requirements of the use of the saddle horse in different eras, these procedures had constituted a coherent ensemble of recipes of recognized efficacy more than a method, properly said.

The old *écuyers* were little concerned with erecting a theory. In an art composed completely of execution, the "how" of their practice preoccupied them more than the "why." They had also probably thought it to be sufficient, not without reason, to demonstrate the movement, or at least to make their horses go.

Baucher, who must have surpassed them all in ability, invented new procedures of a power unknown until then. He justified their effects in theory, built them into principles from which he made a body of doctrine that was the base of a tightly coordinated methodical system. Thus he found it justified to entitle his *"novum organum:" Méthode d'équitation basée sur de nouveaux principes* (*Method of Equitation Based on New Principles*, see Nelson, Hilda, *François Baucher, The Man and his Method*, J. A. Allen, London, 1992).

General l'Hotte, who was Baucher's best student, drew a brilliant portrait of his Master. Many chapters of his works are consecrated to the examination of the theory and practice of the new method. There is no question of contesting the value of the General's judgment; at most, one could aspire to add to his study some details, unknown at the time, that do not seem to be without interest.

Such is the goal that the author has proposed for the present compilation.

Baucher taught equitation from 1823 to 1870. It was only in 1848 that General l'Hotte, then a Lieutenant, met the Master for the first time and assiduously followed his lessons for three months. Over the course of the following ten years, the distance from Paris of his successive postings, the slowness of communications, and the rarity of leave permitted Captain l'Hotte only rare and short visits to his teacher, who was at the time making long tours of other countries. From 1860 to 1864, *Chef d'escadrons* l'Hotte commanded the Cavalry Section at Saint-Cyr, and the proximity to Paris probably allowed him to see Baucher more frequently, but from 1864 to 1870, the duties of *Écuyer en chef* at Saumur were too absorbing to have allowed him to meet with Baucher often or for long. It was evidently the same in 1870 and 1871. After the war, Colonel l'Hotte, Commanding Officer of the 18th Dragoons at Versailles had no lack of chances to visit Baucher, then in his retirement, as often as he was able until Baucher's death in 1873.

In sum, the relationship between master and student was reduced to three months of assiduous daily work and four years of relatively frequent meetings divided over the course of 21 of the 47 years of Baucher's ministry. As well, by the time of last visits of the General, the *Écuyer* had become infirm and blind.

It was certainly from Baucher himself that the General got the recitation of the events that he had not witnessed himself in his Master's life, and it is interesting to put this recitation together with the memories of Baucher's other students who witnessed, and even took part in those events.

The memoirs used for this purpose are those of Louis Rul, clarified and completed by his friend Eugène Caron.

Rul was one of the most curious figures in the Baucherist group of stars. Born in Guadeloupe, very young when brought to Paris where he joyously dissipated the benefits of his paternal plantations. "Handsome as a lightly bronzed god," Théophile Gautier said of him, an artist overflowing with lyricism and fantasy, brilliant conversationalist and biting polemicist, he was connected with all the young Romanticists. He had taken lessons at the *Manège des Pages* from Vicomte O'Hégerty, *écuyer* at Versailles, and, from Baucher's arrival in Paris onward, was a passionate follower of the new method, which he studied in depth. Very gifted in equitation, he became a well-loved disciple of the Master for whom he kept the most respectful attachment all his life. When he had achieved his ruin, he used his equestrian knowledge to make a living, and endowed with the only certificate of perfect orthodoxy that the Master ever bestowed on one of his students, he undertook propaganda tours aboard in favor of the new method. He was, outside of that, a mediocre ambassador. A mainstay of drinking dives and a redoubtable duelist, he was well known by all the police in Europe, and despite his talent, caused more damage to, rather than propagation of, the new gospel.

His friend Caron was quite different. Master of a *Manège* after fourteen years of service in the Cavalry, having become established bourgeois and careful about respect in his community, he had first met Rul at the beginning of the heroic period of Baucherism, when the two of them were initiated into the method.

Their opposite characters even brought them together, and afterwards united them in a long and loyal friendship. It lasted forty years, over the course of which Caron made notes of their memoires, both common and personal.

But Rul had more imagination than memory, and at several year intervals, his recitations of the same events often presented notable differences. Caron's positive and precise mind set itself to establish among the variants, the version of the facts that most approached their reality. Such as he reports them, one can take them as accurate.

Finally, no one in France, it seems, had any knowledge of a brochure written against Baucher and his method, published in Berlin in 1852 by the best *écuyer* in Prussia at that time: Louis Seeger.

Seeger studied Baucher's method with a malevolent blindness, but also with an indisputable competence, and with a rigor of examination of which none of Baucher's French adversaries gave any example.

To the judgment of General l'Hotte, who could not have entirely escaped the influence of his respectful affection for his master, this brochure furnishes a counterpoint strongly influenced in the opposite direction.

It is an element of appreciation that one should not neglect in trying to approach the truth.

General Decarpentry

DEDICATED TO THE MEMORY
Of my grandfather
EUGÈNE CARON
student of Baucher
who founded the Manège de Douai in 1849
and directed it until 1880
and of his son
my uncle
EDOUARD CARON
who succeeded him in the direction of the Manège
until 1914
Civilian hostage in Camp Holzminden
deceased from the effects of his captivity
Knight of the Legion of Honour
posthumously

CHAPTER 1 - THE EARLY YEARS

Baucher rarely spoke of his youth and beginnings. It was not that he sought in the least to conceal his origins that for being modest were no less perfectly honorable, but he was always very reserved about everything that concerned his private life. His father was a butcher in Versailles and probably had a good business, considering that the inheritance that he left his only son François let the son take over a *manège* in Harve in 1822.

François Baucher was born in 1796 on the *Rue des Boucheries*, two steps from the former Royal Stables, the buildings of which had housed the celebrated *Académie d'Équitation de l'Europe* for two centuries. The same year, an "*École Nationale d'Équitation*" was organized in these buildings from the remains of the junior personnel and materiel from the old academy which had been dispersed by the revolutionary storm. Thus from his infancy and during the years of his youth, François Baucher was surely attracted to the daily spectacle of equestrian exercises that played out before his eyes on the terraces around the stables.

One of his uncles, about whom we have no further knowledge, was in the service of Prince Borghese, for whom he managed the stables in Turin. The Prince, part of the imperial family by way of his marriage to Pauline Bonaparte, was named Governor of Piedmont by Napoleon. His household grew according to his new status and his stables were transferred to Milan. The director of the stables came to France from time to time to look for horses, carriages, and personnel.

Returning from one of these remount tours, he brought with him to Milan as a student hunt rider his nephew François who thus began, around 1810, a career in which he would know some brilliant successes and many disappointments. Under the direction of his uncle, the student worked "with an indefatigable ardour," Baucher later told General l'Hotte, and it is probably to this uncle, of whom we know not where he had learned equitation, that Baucher owed his early education.

However, it is not without interest to bring up that an Italian *écuyer* of great reputation, named Mazuchelli,[1] taught at the Milan Academy at this Time. The curious and observant mind of François Baucher probably did not fail to be taken with this academy, home to an art that he was already passionate about, and with the celebrated *écuyer* that directed it.

There is nothing to affirm that Baucher received training from Mazuchelli, and even if the birth of Baucher's talent was influenced by Mazuchelli, we know not in what measure.

At the fall of the Empire, Baucher returned to France, "after having visited the principal *manèges* (of Europe) for his personal instruction," said General l'Hotte. After that he surely stayed at his father's house, considering that later he also recounted to the General his ruses for observing the Vicomte d'Abzac, whose sorties on his horses he watched, and also considering that it was not until 1816 that the Royal School at Versailles was reestablished under the direction of the celebrated Vicomte. Later we find Baucher in the service of the *Duc* de Berry's stables, then, towards 1820, as *écuyer* in Hâvre in the *manège* owned by Monsieur de Chatillon whom he succeeded as director-proprietor. A little later, without abandoning this *manège*, he took over, in Rouen on the Rue Duguay-Trouin, the one that Antoine Franconi had founded there in 1775, and for ten years he directed both establishments simultaneously.

---

1   In his dressage, Mazuchelli pushed to the extreme the minutiae and rigors that the Neopolitan School had spread throughout Italy over the course of the XVIII century. His horses were prepared on the longe and the long lines for a long time with all sorts of auxiliary rein arrangements, worked in hand and in the pillars with the help of numerous aides reinforced by whips, longe whips, and toothed cavessons. It was perhaps to the memory of these complicated and rigorous practices that Baucher owed the horror that he manifested afterwards for the use of "machines" in the training of horses!

What training did Baucher give to his students in Hâvre and Rouen? Were his lessons still those of the classical *manège* conforming to the tradition of the Old School? It was in 1833 that he published his first work, the *"Dictionnaire d'équitation"* (*Dictionary of Equitation*) in which the whole essence of his method is contained and which, from all evidence, had nothing improvised in it. It was surely on the contrary the fruit of lengthy and thorough experimentation and study that required plenty of time. Over the course of the years of preparation of this revolutionary manifesto, had Baucher continued to profess the principles that he rejected in his own work?

It is hardly probable, but we only know that for the instruction of his students, he had not abandoned the use of a "jumper" in the pillars, of which he later denied the utility. He had one in his stables in Rouen, well known by all the horsemen of the region whom the horse had "deposited" without exception on the ground; except one, General l'Hotte tells us. Baucher stayed secure on the horse's back.

CHAPTER II - THE CIRCUS

At the end of the year 1834, Baucher came to Paris and associated himself with Jules-Charles Pellier, Director of the *Manège* de la Rue St-Martin.

Pellier was from an old greatly esteemed family. His great uncle had been one of the personnel at the *Écuries de Versailles* under Louis XV. His uncle, Louis-Charles, emigrated, and served in the Condé household for the whole exile of the Princes.[2] At the Restoration, Louis-Charles had been, under the princes' patronage, named *Écuyer* at the *Manège* Royal de Paris, and he was able to set up his nephew, Jules-Charles, at the *Manège* de la Rue St-Martin to which the protection of the Court had assured a clientele of all the youth of *Faubourg St-Germain*.

Moreover, his good relationship with the personnel of the Royal Stables and the Princes' stables often allowed him to remount his nephew's *manège* advisedly and at good prices from the turnover in these stables.

This happy period came to an end with the Days of July. The fall of the Bourbons not only deprived Pellier of their support, but the personnel at the Écuries d'Orléans were hostile to him,

---

2   As for his father, in the family, they spoke of him as little as possible. After 1815, instead of emigrating, he had flirted with the successive governments of the Revolution. He had preserved his position at the head of the *Manège* de la Rue de Provence, and even received a subsidy from Minister of War Bouchette. He had however the tact to die before the end of the Revolution so that Jules-Charles, upon the return of the Bourbons, could make himself well known as the nephew of his uncle rather than as the son of his father.

and the remount of the *Manège* de la Rue St-Martin no longer benefited from the advantages of the old days.

Furthermore, to add to the ordeal, the Vicomte d'Aure set up a *manège* on the Rue Duphot where he brought together the best horses from the *École de Versailles* that had been auctioned off after the revolution, the surplus thoroughbreds from the racing stables, and some rogues, the owners of whom had not been sorry to get rid of them.

In a short time, and without embracing the formalism of the Old School, d'Aure taught his students to use their mounts of such different types honorably. He had created, in sum, an equitation for *"gens du monde,"* and his success asserted itself day by day.

Deserting Pellier's *Manège*, the youth of Faubourg St-Germain came in crowds to the Rue Duphot to take lessons from the *Écuyer* to whom the renown of Versailles gave great prestige.

In these difficult conditions, Pellier was certainly not going to quarrel with being joined by an associate who brought with him fresh money and the beginning of a reputation.

It was on Rue St-Martin that Baucher found his first disciples, Pellier himself at first, then Maxime Gaussen and Rul.

Their winning-over marked a stage on the way on which he was engaged. Through Pellier, he reached a place in the much closed body of the association of *Maîtres de Manège*, little inclined to novelty, and through Gaussen, he reached the rich and cultivated bourgeoisie. As to Rul, he was due to become a tireless propagandist for the method and a loyal friend in the face of every test.

It was also on Rue St-Martin that Baucher first trained the horses that would make him celebrated, Partisan and Captaine in particular.

The *Manège* then had a revival of activity, but Pellier did not believe that he had to be content with that, and, without abandoning his first establishment, he wanted to extend his business by taking over, with Laurent Franconi, a circus *manège* that was folding in Pecq. This circus had been mounted at the time of the inauguration of the St-Germain railway, and the affluence of the public that was taken by this novelty had for a while filled the director's till. Then a slump came with the end of the Parisians' infatuation with the railway.

However, even if the exploitation of the shows was deficient, the rental of horses for the promenade in the *Bois de St-Germain* remained profitable, and the demand exceeded the effective strength of the stables. Pellier, who had on the other hand too many horses in Paris for the clients that had remained with him, counted on finding a way to make the horses earn their oats there in Pecq.

Baucher bowed to these peremptory factors in the commercial order and associated himself with Franconi at the same time as did Pellier for the revival of this second *manège*.

Laurent Franconi was a figure in Paris and the most experienced specialist in matters of the circus. He was moreover a true *écuyer*, and with him, *Haute École* entered the *piste*, where before they had only presented dressage at liberty, vaulting, or equestrian ballets. Without his championing it, the public saw in him a representative of old French equitation and confused him with the survivors of the École de Versailles, even though that he had nothing in common with it.

Venetian in origin, but having come at a very young age to France with his father, Franconi had probably been trained by him, a student of the celebrated Italian *Écuyer*, Mazuchelli, whom Baucher surely had not failed to admire when he was attached to Prince Borghese's stables in Milan.

So Baucher, who found in Franconi the son of the former director of his *Manège* de Rouen, had something in common with him, not counting equestrian talent and a solid amity was born between the two artists that neither time nor rivalry ever touched.

Franconi was struck by the variety of Baucher's horses' work that far surpassed the narrowly classical, to which the old *écuyer* remained loyal. Since he was twenty years older than his colleague and felt himself getting old, he had the wisdom not to take umbrage at this natural born superiority, but to the contrary he set himself to help his young colleague in his pursuit of notoriety. It was he who succeeded in making Baucher decide to launch his career as a circus *écuyer*, where the innovator had so far made only a few little remarkable appearances.

Baucher probably was too touchy to be able accept patronage that he perhaps had not otherwise needed. Certainly he even found it difficult to admit to having a godfather, but he would go on to find in Franconi his most qualified introduction into a milieu where he knew nearly no one, and his wisest counselor for the practice of his new profession.

Franconi knew all the circus troupes, some of whom he had often directed himself, and their directors, such as Dejean and Soullié. The demands of the public were not a secret to him. Moreover, to the irritation of Pellier, the coming to power of the d'Orléans had pulled him, Pellier, into a difficult period. Bonaparte, in fact, had in the past conferred on him the riding instruction of the *Vélites de la Garde Consulaire*. Franconi also had, in the person of Prince Eugène de Beauharnais, an excellent student to whom he remained strongly attached. All that had not put him into the good graces of the *Ultras*,[3] who gave him the evil eye. On the contrary, the new court brought honor back to the followers of the Imperial regime and Franconi was too adroit not to know how to profit from that.

In 1835, Adolphe Franconi, brother of Laurent, and his associate, Dejean, obtained authorization to erect a circus tent on the Champs-Élysées, at the entrance to "*Carré Marigny*," in the place where there would later be a theatre of the same name.

Three years later, the tent gave way to a circus made of wood, and in 1840, the City of Paris constructed a circus in stone, monumental for that era, at the other end of "*Carré Marigny*," almost at the edge of Avenue Matignon. Adolphe Franconi remained the concessionaire and it was there that Baucher went on to come by his brilliant reputation.

It is difficult, a hundred years later (in 1948), to describe the place that the circus held in Parisian life at the time Baucher was about to make his entrance there.

---

3   The ultra conservatives

Inaugurated in France only a few years before the Revolution, the circus remained a popular spectacle for a long time, but disdained by high society and even little frequented by the middle class.

After 1830, its popularity grew ceaselessly. The bourgeois, great and small, happily spent their evenings there, and the elegant world began to flock there. Soon the loges were rented for the season like those in the theatre and the Duc d'Orléans himself gave an example as soon as the stone-built circus opened its doors.

For the *"gentleman"* who came to succeed the *"gentilhomme"* in the social order, it became high-toned to be seen as regularly at the Circus as at the Races and to pass for an enlightened fan of "Equestrian Games," as they still say today, as well as the performances on the Turf.

On Opening Nights, from which the Directors of the Theatre took count to plan their programs, one could see members of the young Jockey Club, the horsemen of Paris, and representatives of the press at the stage door.

Society news and gossip went on at length about the quality of the show, the curves of the *écuyères*, and the brilliant line-up of the public. In the *"Debats,"* Jules Janin celebrated now the physique of Madame Lejars, who had served as the model for the sculpted *amazone*[4] at the front of the Circus, now the charms of a female equilibrist, or now made the readers shudder at the description of a *"Salto Mortale"* executed by the celebrated Auriol.

The circus was on an elegant Parisian street, it had solidified its place among the gatherings of society as a good place to be seen, and it would keep that place for more than fifty years.

The horse played an essential role in the show. Outside of some presentations by acrobats and jugglers, it figured in all the numbers in the programme, whether as the principal element in *Haute École* and the work at liberty, or as a premier figure in "contra-dances, *pas de deux* and *pas de quatre*, or ballets executed

---

4   Lady rider

by costumed Artists," or again as the indispensable accessory in the vaulting exercises.

The privilege of "last number," always reserved for the stars, was invariably consecrated to *Haute École*. The elegant people often had retired to the back of their loges, disdaining the final pantomime, which on the contrary delighted the greater public, little spoiled in their taste for the comic because clowns were rare and *Auguste*[5] had not yet been invented.

Adolphe Franconi, counseled by his brother, gladly hired Baucher. The way to success was thus open to the great artist, but it was not without obstacles.

To conquer the public, he had to surmount the prestige, by then becoming old, of Laurent Franconi, and the charm of "Caroline," incontestably the queen of the *piste*.

Happily for Baucher, Franconi hardly did any School dressage, and his old mare Norma was too well known by the Parisians who grew quickly weary of everything. Franconi reserved the mare for tours of the provinces, and he appeared much less in performances on the Champs-Élysées. This semi-retirement allowed Baucher to avoid comparisons from which his lack of presence might run the risk of suffering beside the elegant correctness of Franconi whom they called "majesty on a horse."

As to Caroline Loyo, she was a very pretty woman and the first *amazone* to present a School horse at the circus. This horse had been trained for her by L. C. Pellier who then taught her to ride him. She did it not without cleverness but without great concern for the traditions to which her old master was so attached. He severely rebuked the extravagances of his pupil who, in contrast to him, had won the favors of the profane crowd. She had great skill in the art of seducing spectators and took advantage of it with exhilaration. Won over by her brio, the connoisseurs accorded her amused indulgence. Her admirers showered her with cheers and flowers, and the greater public gave her ovations and demanded interminable curtain calls and

---

5   The least intelligent type of clown with exaggerated features

encores. Jules Janin called her "the equestrian Taglioni" and he never ran out of rave reviews of his subject.

Of course, she had the privilege of the last number. There could be no question of taking it away from her, while Baucher, on his part, would not stand for appearing before her. With their customary adroitness, the Franconis answered this thorny question in no time at all. The two artists would each have their night alternatively when the other would not appear and they could thus enjoy the privilege of not having to quarrel.

Moreover, Baucher showed himself just as clever as his directors. Caroline had bought from Lord Seymour a Thoroughbred named "*Fortunatus*"[6] and had undertaken his training, but the horse was too difficult for her youthful experience, and she voluntarily ceded him to Baucher who discreetly trained the horse and sold him "*fin prêt*" at a friendly price back to the vivacious écuyère.

From then on Caroline was won over. She had to take some lessons from Baucher to learn how to present the horse. From then on she consented to be counted among his students but without Baucher being able to take great satisfaction because she remained just as obedient to the counsel of the second as to the first of her masters. Nothing could prevent her from lashing the unfortunate "*Fortunatus*" with a great whack of the whip when she encountered the gaze of one of her enemies in the audience, and her escapades had brought her a certain number of them who, in a nasty play on words, called her, while sniggering, "*La Loyo*" in allusion to the abundance of her charms, for all that, ample in the style of the times.

Finally all rivalry disappeared when Caroline accepted a lucrative engagement in London. She would still have more acclaim there than in Paris and from then on leave Baucher to reign over the *piste* in the Champs-Élysées.

He certainly must have felt great satisfaction because he had gotten to the goal that he had pursued over the years, but

---

6   General l'Hotte reported another anecdote about a Fortunatus also owned by Lord Seymour. It does not seem to have been the same horse.

his morose and unquiet character took the upper hand when someone congratulated him, and he responded bitterly, "It's true. I live with the acrobats, and I am seen for ten *Sous*." This did not prevent him from responding with hauteur to a rude detractor who called him a *"baladin,"* "Shakespeare and Molière had no fear of playing themselves in their works." Perhaps he dreamed of a great School, of a new Versailles, where his teaching would receive all the development that it merited.

Still he was going to be able to compel the attention of the public and to oblige all riders of good faith to recognize the power of the equestrian means that he had invented, as well as the perfection of the results that they allowed him to obtain.

For fifteen years, in Paris, Berlin, Vienna, Milan, and Venice, he went on to demonstrate the unequaled value of his new method by his brilliant success.

But the same style of propaganda realized by his engagement at the circus could not fail to act on the putting into practice of his method. From then on, all his preoccupations came to concentrate on the tight circle of the *piste*, on the execution of a series of tours de force gathered into a quarter of an hour. "What could be the most can be the least," he probably thought, but practical equitation, the daily usage of the horse, military or civilian, was not the "least" that he believed necessarily contained the "most" of spectacular equitation; it was "something else," and Montigny[7], celebrating the Second Manner of the Master 30 years later, had reason to say that the "most" was doubtlessly perfect, but for only 10 minutes of presentation within the walls of the circus.

Baucher's success asserted itself from night to night. Aubert[8] and the *Versaillais*[9] often joked from time to time about his "lack of manners," but the Vicomte d'Aure himself, who showed

---

7   Distinguished *écuyer* (See p. 1).

8   Aubert, civilian *écuyer* of great reputation.

9   This was the name used for the *écuyers* and *piqueurs* from the old and celebrated École Royale de Versailles, nearly two centuries old at the Revolution, done away with by it, reestablished in 1815, and disbanded again in 1830. The Vicomte d'Aure was the most outstanding personality of these personnel.

more ease than correctness on a horse, consented to applaud with the tips of his fingers. The elegant world let themselves be won over, and the greater public was captured. Jules Janin reported on the new star of the *piste* with all the enthusiasm that he had manifested for Caroline, and celebrated in the same ink the virtuosity of the artist who, he wrote in all innocence, made his horse change leg "at all the gaits."

But in 1842, Baucher published his *"Méthode d'équitation basée sur de nouveaux principes"* (*Method of Equitation Based on New Principles*, see Hilda Nelson, *François Baucher, the Man and his Method*, J. A. Allen, London, 1992). No one had read his *"Dictionnaire d'équitation"* (*Dictionary of Equitation*) that had appeared in Rouen in 1833 under his name, then totally unknown. The *"Dialogues sur l'équitation"* (1834) (*Dialogues on Equitation*, see Nelson), *"Le Résumé complet des principes de la nouvelle méthode"* (1837) (*Complete Resumé of the Principles of the New Method"*), *"Passe-temps équestres"* (1840) (*Equestrian Pastimes*) had not gone beyond the circle of the habitués of the *Manège*-Pellier.

This time, the name of the author alone sufficed for someone to grab the new work, so much so that a second edition had to follow the first after an interval of only three months, and two more in the same year. Reading it could only profoundly irritate all the horsemen educated in the traditional school, that is to say the immense majority of them.

"I say openly," wrote Baucher, "that the *rassembler* has never been understood nor defined before me..." and he ridiculed "the routine and the prejudgments" of his predecessors in equestrian art. How could the masters and students of Versailles not rear up before such intemperate attacks on the objects of their righteous veneration?!

The public was soon divided into two very heated camps... At the circus, the innovator's faithful followers heightened the tone of their acclamation further, and his detractors that of their taunts.

The Vicomte d'Aure took the part of head of the defenders of the faith, and published *"Observations sur la nouvelle Méthode d'équitation"* (*Observations on the New Method of Equitation*).

Behind him were lined up, among the professionals, the Master of the *Manèges* of Luxembourg and the Rue Duphot, along with those of Rues Saint-Martin and Saint-Cécile. Pellier and de Fitte had definitely passed into the ranks of Baucher disciples. The Faubourg Saint-Germain, the sons of which were taking lessons from the Vicomte, now showed a cold scorn at the performances at the circus. The Jockey Club affected holding themselves above the quarrel, but Lord Seymour was inclined toward the d'Aurists while the *Comte* de Miramon became one of Baucher's best students, and Monsieur Mackenzie-Grieves, renown steeplechaser, also came to take lessons from the innovator.

The world of letters and that of the arts were not less divided. Lamartine visited Baucher on Rue Saint-Martin, while Alexandre Dumas, member of the Club Équestre de Luxembourg, lined up on the side of the traditionalists, abandoned by Eugène Sue and Delacroix.

The Court itself took part! But harmony did not reign at Tuileries either. The Duc d'Orléans went to see Baucher work many times, while the Duc de Nemours, student of Vicomte d'Aure, voluntarily took up opinions opposite to his elder brother and lined up under the banner of his master. As to the greater public, it opted en masse for Baucher against the traditionalists that it irreverently called *"les perruques"* (the wigs.) Equestrian art, without a doubt, did not play a great part in the determination of the public's choice, and politics did not fail to be introduced into the quarrel. It pleased the bourgeois and the *"Héros de Juillet"*[10] to acclaim a "son of the people" who had come to mastery without masters and to *faire le nique*[11] at the surviving "emigrants" of Versailles.

Baucher's name no longer appeared in *"les Débats."* It was the "National" that now sang his praises. Clement Thomas[12] was naturally in the innovator's camp, and Lafitte, the banker, left behind in his liberalism, went to the opposite camp.

---

10   Sympathizers to the three day revolution of 1830
11   A sign of contempt, to mock
12   The future General of the Garde Nationale, shot in 1871 by the *Communards*

Baucher on Partisan

To pamphlets published against Baucher, responded those of his partisans with a tone not any less acerbic. They affected the style of writing "Monsieur Daure" without the apostrophe to designate the Vicomte, and the new method was gladly presented as one of the conquests of the "Trois Glorieuses."

The army kept to a prudent reserve, but its attention was aroused. It was not by chance that in the "new method," all the riders in the pictures are wearing cavalry uniforms. In performances at the circus, Baucher abandoned his costumes inspired by those of the *Écuyers* at Versailles for dress of a military cut and aspect. The circus for him was just a process for publicity of the method that he wanted to introduce into the army.

This skillful detour did not escape the perception of his adversaries, and the wiser among them, beginning with the Vicomte d'Aure, were very careful in contesting the spectacular success of the artist. They simply but firmly refused to acknowledge any practical value in his new method for everyday equitation, such as that called for in the military use of the horse.

Their opinion was shared by many authorities in the cavalry, and Baucher would have had little chance to arrive at his goals if he did not have the good fortune to win to his cause General Oudinot, who introduced him to the army the way that Franconi had introduced him to the circus.

General Oudinot was rightly considered one of the best riders in the army and enjoyed great prestige in the cavalry. He had commanded the school at Saumur for five years in difficult conditions and had been perfectly successful, as much from a political point of view as from a military and equestrian point of view.[13]

Subsequently attaché to the Duc d'Orléans, who showed him an amiable confidence, he thought of getting the Prince's atten-

13   After General Berton's conspiracy in 1822, the School had been dissolved, then reestablished at Versailles, and reconstituted at Saumur only in 1825. It was General Oudinot who had been in charge of this reorganization made delicate by the persistence of liberal agitation amongst the Saumurois, and by the malcontent of the military following the repression from the Berton affair. The General Oudinot's tact and firmness had assured order and calm in the School, and contributed to the pacification of spirits in the region. For the instruction, his authority had put an end to the discord in the military and equestrian training. Under his firm authority, the commission charged with their indispensable unification had terminated the "Course of Military Equitation" which settled old quarrels. Finally, work in the outdoor arena, which had been very little part of the equestrian instruction until then, was largely developed by him, and favored by the adoption of the English saddle still nearly unknown by the military of that era. Obtained after a long insistence to the authorities in the cavalry, this fortunate innovation brought a new appeal to exterior work, and the officers rightly attributed that all to the merit of the General.

tion to Baucher's new theories and the extraordinary results that their author had obtained.

The Prince, who had already received lessons from Franconi earlier, was in a position to appreciate the great difficulty of the equestrian tours de force by the innovator and he gladly recognized the value of the method that allowed Baucher to perform them. But the arguments of those who declared it inapplicable in the army did not appear to him to be without foundation.

Over the course of his campaigns in Algeria, the Prince had been able, within the constraints of military equitation, to put his finger on the limit of the demands that it could impose on riders as well as on the horses. The suggestion that General Oudinot had made in view of an official experiment in the new method in the cavalry left him perplexed. To overcome his hesitations required a decisive test, and it was Lord Seymour that without premeditation furnished the occasion.

In his stables, Lord Seymour had a three year old Thoroughbred colt named "Géricault" that was rebellious and violent in his defenses to the point that no one could stay on him. Always very "sport," Géricault's owner made it known that he would offer the horse to any rider able to make a tour of the *Bois* (de Boulogne) on his back without being thrown.

Of course this novel proposition, very much in the manner of its author, was soon the object of all conversation in the equestrian milieu and it excited the rivalry between the d'Aurists and the Baucherists.

Among the first was the Vicomte de Tournon, considered the most vigorous student of Vicomte d'Aure, agreed to take up the challenge and failed in his enterprise. In the name of the disciples of the new School, the Comte Lancosme-Brèves[14] in turn tried the test and succeeded.

The Baucherists were loudly triumphant, even a little bit more than they had coming to them. Their adversaries observed right away, and not without reason, that the winner of the fight

---

14 Lancosme-Brèves, écuyer and distinguished equestrian writer, was inclined to decisive judgments doctorally expressed.

was a transfer from the Old School recently converted to the new. They were justified in claiming that the power of his position and seat most surely resulted from training received over long years under the direction of the Vicomte d'Aure, rather then a few months spent in the Rue Saint-Martin. Then, and more importantly, they contested the value of his success, realized according to the letter of the bet more than in its spirit.

Because, while Monsieur de Tournon had undertaken the battle alone, without recourse to any other help than his own means of seat and use of his aids, things were not the same for Monsieur de Brèves. The "renegade" had in effect met the test well, but under conditions that made it infinitely less difficult. A large group of rider friends had surrounded Géricault as soon as he was mounted, tightening closely, even bumping up against him, to the point of leading him forward whether he liked it or not, without for a single moment leaving him the possibility of executing any defense that he might know well enough to make use of. Truthfully, success had been conjured up.

Even though nothing really had been proven for or against the new method; the public, not knowing the details of the affair and not having seen it up close, chanted victory with the Baucherists.

Lord Seymour, always a good player, sent Géricault to M. de Brèves who immediately paid homage to his master. Baucher, accepting the praise, announced that he would present the horse at the Circus "later, in six weeks." This time, the value of the new method and the reputation of its author really came into play!

Would Géricault's training present serious difficulties? Nobody knew a thing. The horse was *rétif* (stubborn) and violent, but he was not *méchant* (nasty, bad) nor fearful. It was not likely that he would surrender without some fights after the long series of victories that he had had over successive riders, and the legend of Baucher's lack of solidity in the saddle held up very little more likelihood. In any case, the Master's tact and methodical address without any doubt played an infinitely more important role than did the solidity of his seat in the domination of Géricault.

"Who then has seen a horse defend himself under Baucher?" wrote General l'Hotte, and he added, "Me, never."

As always, the Master, who did not easily let himself be interrogated, spoke to no one, not even to his preferred students. They knew from the personnel at the *manège* that he worked Géricault several times a day, very early in the morning and very late at night, that he saddled and bridled him himself, without admitting the presence of any aide, and that, toward the end of the training, he had ridden the horse many times in the circus *piste*, chandeliers alight, with the sound of the orchestra.

Of course, the damnedest rumors ran through the public, especially among the adversaries. Sometimes it was that Baucher had fascinated Géricault by mysterious procedures, or even put him to sleep with soporific drugs, sometimes that he had deprived the horse of food, water, and sleep.

Baucher let them talk, and pursued his training. At the end of the third week, the rumors ran that Géricault would be presented "very shortly," and in the first days of the following week, the National announced to its readers that "Monsieur Baucher will present at the Friday Opening Night, Géricault, the horse reputed to be untameable, well known amongst all the riders of Paris."

In the salons as well as in the *Bois*, in the *manèges* as well as at the Races, the story of the day was commented on passionately. The unshakable faith of the Master's young students celebrated a brilliant success in advance, but the more experienced among them were not without some inquietude about the results of such precipitated training and about the unknown factors in an assuredly adventurous presentation.

The risk of failure had no more escaped the method's adversaries, for whom the possibility, if not the likelihood, of a failure was not to be deplored.

Origines de l'École de Cavalerie
(Origins of the École de Cavalerie *after Adam*)

On Opening Night, the Circus was jam-packed. The cohort of Baucher loyalists was pressed up to the stage door. There, Rul was holding forth with extravagant gestures. The Baron de Curnieu[15] launched witticisms, and Lancosme-Brèves, some maxims.

There appeared in the foreground, General Oudinot who appeared worried, Got, the actor from the Comédie Française, Eugène Sue, Delacroix, and Théophile Gautier, for whom his corpulence by then prohibited riding... but he had again worn for these circumstances the celebrated scarlet waistcoat that he had worn twelve years before at the Battle of Hernani... (*Translator's note:* actually a confrontation between classists and romantics at the Comédie Française at a performance of "Hernani.")

Around in front, facing them, at the public entrance, were grouped the *"perruques."* Jardin, Coupé, Lançon, Bellanger, all the former staff from Versailles and the *Manège* Royal de Paris were lined up behind the Vicomte d'Aure who, perhaps a little more frequently than was customary, drew upon his snuffbox. In his clear voice with its Outre-Garonne accent, he conversed with Aubert, who listened to him devotedly. Beside them, the Vicomte de Touron, who had suffered another of his falls, supported himself on his cane.

In the d'Orléans loge, the Duchess was installed with her two sons, but the Duc was absent. The public distractedly applauded the artists' shortened numbers.

Auriol, king of the trampoline, who presented his vaulting just before Baucher's entrance, was about to polish off his perilous jumps when the Duc discreetly entered his loge, waving away marks of respect by those in attendance. General Oudinot's visage became serene, and that of Vicomte d'Aure, somber.

Finally, Baucher made his entrance, in absolute silence. His dress looked as if it might be mistaken for that of a staff officer of the *Garde Nationale,* so dear to the Parisians, and he had added a cavalry sabre. Géricault advanced at a walk that was a little precipitated, but straight and firm, up to the middle of the

---

15 Baron Le Curnieu. Distinguished horseman and hippologist, known for his witticisms.

piste where Baucher kept him immobile while with his bicorn hat with cock feathers, he saluted the spectators with a circular gesture, stopping for a long moment before the d'Orléans loge.

Then a storm of applause exploded while the orchestra started a military march. Géricault knowingly took the *piste*, showing more surprise than fear and without manifesting the least attempt at resistance.

Baucher made him do some simple but perfectly correct work visibly inspired by military regulations. Little by little, he loosened the constraint that had at first assured the domination of the horse. Géricault relaxed his gaits, described voltes and half-passes without being disturbed by the public or the music or the clicking of the sabre against the spur.

Short halts and instantaneous departs in turn broke up and reestablished the work at the canter, at first flowing, and then little by little cadenced for the execution of pirouettes, and finally lengthened as much as the dimensions of the *piste* would allow. Two changes of hand with flying changes of lead finished the work.

On the last *doublé*, at the artists' entryway, Géricault halted in a *parade-éclair*, and this time Baucher saluted with all the confidence that he so often lacked. A delirious ovation accompanied his exit, executed in a rein back (not anticipated) of majestic amplitude.

To clear the passageway, the Baucherist phalanx had overflowed onto the *piste*. In the racket, one could see Théophile Gautier brandishing his hat. Rul fussed around the Master, and all the faithful appeared struck with frenzy.

Facing them in the suddenly brightened up ranks of the d'Aurists, Vicomte de Tournon, cane under his arm, applauded and cheered, while the Vicomte d'Aure put less passion into imitating him.

After a call-back, in which Baucher appeared on foot, somewhat tangled up in his sabre, the orchestra attacked the "Parisienne," somewhat forgotten since 1839, but that well marked the public's feeling for the success of the New School.

With it the liberals and the romantics triumphed. The defeat of the *"perruques"* was consummated by this definitive victory in the test that Rul's bombast had already baptized "the Second Battle of Hernani." The Duc d'Orléans had made his decision. Baucher had achieved his ends.

Baucher riding Capitaine at the Franconi Circus in front of Commandant de Novital, with (left to right) L'Hotte, Caroline Loya, and Franconi watching. Gouache and crayon drawing by Commandant Margot. (courtesy G. Margot)

CHAPTER III - BAUCHER: THE MAN, THE ÉCUYER, THE WRITER

What contents in this new method revolutionized the equestrian world?

Before explaining, it would seem useful to trace, as exactly as the memories of contemporaries permit, a physical and mental portrait of its author whose personality appears to have been captivating to all those who came near him.

Baucher had a great deal of natural distinction. His countenance captured the eye and the whole of his features radiated sensitivity. His eyes, very long under eyelids that were a bit heavy, became very animated during conversation, and especially in the heat of his teaching, for which he had a great passion.

His chest, a bit massive, made him appear a little smaller than his actual size, which was not more than average. Although short, his neck was often flexed under the weight of a somewhat voluminous head. His chest was largely open, and the pronounced camber of his lower back pushed it forward at the same time that it pulled his pelvis backward.

In city clothes, in which Baucher was always dressed with great care, these physical imperfections were barely visible. The ample skirts of the frock coat concealed the thickness of the thighs, very fleshy up to the waist. On horseback, the dress of the time also included the frock coat, and Baucher retained the same advantages as on foot. But in the Circus, he generally wore very fitted costumes, whether in the dress of an academic model (as at Versailles) or that of a military cut. The large hats, often fitted with plumes, forced the abandonment of his head already inclined towards his chest. The tailcoat made his torso thrust out more, and the separation of the skirts sometimes without discretion uncovered the muscular development of his seat, emphasized by the whiteness of the tight fitting pants.

By his physical conformation, Baucher was far from the svelte elegance so prized by the old *écuyers*. It rarely affected his work. Were the grapes perhaps a little green? *(Translator's note: From Aesop's or La Fontaine's fable where a starving fox living under a trellis filled with rosy grapes will not eat them because they are too green and fit only for cads.)*

Correctness was often lacking in the saddle and his position frequently left something to be desired. He neglected it in his work, completely absorbed by the observation of his horse. During the period when, as he himself recognized later, he "abused" the spur, his legs stayed constantly "*plaquées*" (jammed) and carried so far back that his chest fell forward where the weight of his head was already pulling, inclining it in the same direction. In public, he watched himself more and began his presentations correctly after a salute that however always remained quite gauche, despite the exhortations of Franconi. Then, when the difficulties of execution grew with the complication of the work and called as much for nimbleness as precision in the use of the aids, his natural bad habits regained the upper hand and gravely altered correctness.

The supporters of Versailles of course found these faults to be ample material for jokes. "He has his butt for a coat hanger," snickered Aubert. "He blows his nose in his waistcoat," scoffed Lanson. As to the *écuyers* in Berlin, they reproached Baucher's carriage of his head, as they did that of his horse, placed, they said, "as if searching for truffles," and claimed that his spurs "were caught in his horse's coat."

From a moral point of view, Baucher's perfect honesty formed the principal trait of his character. His friends, his students, all those who had come close enough to be able to judge, were unanimous on this subject, and the accusations of plagiarism, brought against him by insinuation more than by affirmation, could not stand up to examination.

This fundamental honesty was accompanied sometimes by an offensive rudeness for those who maladroitly tried to produce their evidence (in an argument).

Baucher was nonetheless disinterested. He had what he needed to live and never sought to make a fortune. In business, he showed himself accommodating to the point of bringing on the reproach of his associates who also judged no less excessive his generosity, a little lavish towards the personnel of the circus and the *manège*.

He was of nearly unhealthy sensibility and susceptibility.

The least attention to him went to his heart and he never forgot it. But the simple suspicion of a malevolent intention toward him never left his memory.

The admiration of the uninformed got on his nerves and he only ever sought it as an evil necessary to the propagation of his method, but felicitations from someone competent were always agreeable to him even if he had to defend his point of view.

Very withdrawn toward strangers and those who were indifferent, on the other hand Baucher loved to confide in his intimate friends who were always of very small number. His touchy and unquiet character portrayed him as believing himself willfully persecuted and the victim of machinations. He vented bitterly in his conversations with his rare confidants.

"The amplitude of Baucher's intelligence," said General l'Hotte, "and the rectitude of his judgment would have made a remarkable man whatever would have been the direction given to his faculties."

He possessed the highest degree of the gift of observation and that of an exploiter of results. He excelled at connecting from effect back to cause with a nearly infallible diagnostic surety. His inventive imagination was inexhaustible. The infinite variety of means that he discovered and used allowed him to say with just cause, "In equitation, I have tried everything," and in fact no one has invented anything notable after him.

The experiments that he put together for his discoveries were conducted with the most precise method and with their application pushed to its absolute limits with an inflexible rigor. He rejected a great number of his new means after having adopted them for some time. Often, the cause of these abandonings resided in the persistent difficulty experienced by his students over the course of the application of a new procedure, but always and over all, it was the concern for better, the infinite pursuit of ideal perfection that decided abandonment or not, as it is for all great artists.

His teaching was luminous. The procedures that he used were no less varied than those that he used in dressage. He proceeded through the study of each student just as he did for each horse, and his penetrating discernment showed itself to be no less acute. In a few hours, the new disciple's character and the form of his mind, as well as his equestrian aptitudes and his receptivity, left nothing unknown to the Master, and he adroitly adapted the form of his lessons to his findings.

Sober in his words with some, on the contrary with others; he developed his explanations through to the smallest details. Sometimes by the precision of terms, sometimes by the originality of the most imaginative formulae and the most ingenious comparisons, he knew how to strike their mind, to fix their attention, and to provoke their reflection. He excelled over all in developing their tact, describing minutely, and in a form adapted to the temperament of each of them, the nature of the sensations that before, they had perceived only vaguely.

He willingly left to find their own way those whom he judged had the aptitude sufficient that they no risk of losing their way, and he knew, at the very moment, when their searching was on the point of success, when to clarify in a single luminous word, the final result that he was helping them to attain[16].

---

16 Entirely in accord between themselves on this point, Rul and Caron are not so with General l'Hotte, who insists on the contrary on Baucher's "conciseness" in his teaching. This divergence is explained by the fact that the extraordinary equestrian aptitude of the General was probably ranked by Baucher in the category of the students that he "left to seek." On the other hand, the General was not able to assist as a spectator at a great number of lessons given by the master. His professional activities did not permit it. On the contrary, Rul and

It is difficult to judge Baucher as a writer because of the ignorance in which we remain on the exact part played by his known and unknown collaborators in the writing of his works.

For his correspondence, his son Henri often served as his secretary, but certain of his letters are undoubtedly by his own hand, and their style is clear, simple, and correct, like that of *"Dictionnaire d'équitation"* (*Dictionary of Equitation*) written in Rouen in 1833, before Baucher came to Paris.

It went completely otherwise in his last *Œuvres Complètes* (*Complete Works*). In contrast, their didactic quality often lacks clarity and precision. In dissertations of a philosophical pretension in which one could regret that he indulged, the bombast too often rivaled an obscurity that was nearly prophetic. Among his collaborators, his associate, Pellier, seems to have been the earliest. In his personal writings, Pellier was not always of a dazzling clarity and his style was without research and often even negligent. So it is not to Pellier then that we must attribute the romantic turgidity of *"Dialogues sur l'équitation"* (*Dialogues on Equitation*, see Nelson), where the great *Hippo-Théo* pompously arbitrates the differences between rider and horse, nor the aphorisms, sometimes hardly intelligible, of *"Passe-Temps équestres"* (*Equestrian Pastimes*), where, anyway, the collaboration of Pellier is even less certain.

It would be necessary to let Baucher take responsibility for this grandiloquence and obfuscation if the influence of Leon

---

Caron, Rul especially, who had spent years in the immediate and permanent entourage of Baucher, had been able to exercise their observation on lessons given to a great number of diversely gifted riders.

Finally, one can not forget that General l'Hotte, so admirably gifted as an executor, was a great deal less so as a teacher. "He did not extend himself," wrote General de la Lance, placed under l'Hotte's orders as a Lieutenant in the 1st Cuir where his cold and reserved character ruined his teaching and "he made few students." In reality, the conciseness that he used in so many cases confined him to mutism so well that "the evil minds" in the *École de Cavalerie* went so far as to call their *Écuyer en Chef "in petto"*, "the light under the bushel." (Trans. note: To put under a bushel is to keep secret.)

Gatayes, their friend in common, were not almost manifest in the excessive style of the two collaborators. Distinguished musician and composer, Gatayes in addition was a chronicler appreciated by the Parisienne Press. To extol the new method of equitation and its author, he rivaled Jules Janin for fanfares. His articles did not often lack spirit, but always simplicity. In not lending but to the rich, one can suspect him to have gracelessly inspired the authors of *Dialogues* and *Passe-Temps*, which, in addition, were dedicated to him.

For the writing of the *Méthode* that appeared in 1842, the celebrated author Got said in his journal that he had been chosen by Baucher as a *"teinturier."*[17] It was a very singular choice! A student at the conservatory, Got was hardly twenty years old. He had ridden for only a few months, less than six under Baucher's direction. To confide in a neophyte, so greatly inexperienced as a rider and as a writer, the revision and correction of twenty years of work and reflection was of a light-handedness hardly believable on the part of Baucher who was already past fifty. Even if the Master had not succeeded in giving to his precepts all the clarity that they called for, one could think that the student, hardly fathoming their meaning, could only contribute to obscuring it.

It is true that the length of the days hardly sufficed to allow the Master to finish the crushing work of his training and lessons, but all of his evenings, General l'Hotte tells us, outside of the two weekly performances at the circus, were "consecrated to work in the office" and "three or four hours of sleep were sufficient for him." So it was not for lack of time that Baucher resorted to collaboration with so astonishing persistence. One is driven to think that he lacked confidence in his aptitude to express in writing what he explained orally with such clarity.

Twenty years after the first edition of his method, when he then modified it profoundly by the adoption of the procedures of his "Second Manner," it was probably this same worry again that drove him to charge five of his students – really qualified

---

[17] That is to say, according to Larrouse, as a "writer that reviews and corrects the works of another."

this time – with writing up, each one separately, an explanation of the last perfections that he had come to teach them in the *manège*. In the twelfth edition of the method, three of these five versions that had not been obviously any less successful (than the others) appeared after the one that Baucher himself wrote. None of them were superior to his; far from it.

In summary, even if, in the words of those that received them, the Master's oral lessons were of brilliant clarity; his written teaching has on the contrary a grave lack of this essential quality. The collaborations, to which he so obstinately returned, without any necessity appearing to impose it, gave only poor results. The text of the method often remains obscure to the point of provoking, in its application by those that had no other guide, errors of interpretation and misunderstanding that have driven them to the worst of disappointments. In other countries especially, where the translation treatments added still more to the obscurity of the original text, the failure of the method was due in large part to its defective editing. Even in France, all of Baucher's good students, struck doubtlessly by its disaccord with the text that had been published by the Master, believed it necessary to write a personal edition of the oral teaching that they had so perfectly assimilated. Yet one must observe that the contract that Baucher had with his publishers permitted them as many new editions of his work as they wanted. Even while the method evolved continually, it was always his early text that was published, without Baucher having had the time – or the right – to modify it. Now, as the recipients of his oral teaching, and the possibility of receiving their lessons directly, have disappeared with the passage of time, recourse to his students' works, more than to his own, has been imposed on those riders concerned with learning and understanding the Master's thinking and the true spirit of his method, because, in Baucher's work, the writer had wronged the *écuyer*.

Caricature by Lorentz
(in the Musée Philipon)

CHAPTER IV - THE PRINCIPLE OF THE METHOD

The principle of Baucher's method is enunciated in his famous formula: "Destroy the instinctive forces, substitute them with transmitted forces."

"By 'force,'" said Baucher, "I mean the motive power that results from muscular contraction; by 'instinctive forces,' those that come from the horse, that is to say, those of which the horse determines the use; by 'transmitted forces,' those that emanate from the rider, and are immediately appreciated by the horse." (*Dictionnaire d'équitation*, 1833) (*Dictionary of Equitation*)

Thus formulated, Baucher's principle necessarily had to raise criticism, and it did give a good hand to the adversaries of the method. The Comte d'Aure, Aubert, and Flandrin[18] were not lacking in rude attack:

- They said, how could instinctive forces be destroyed, other than by death?
- Did it apply then to a stop imposed on their production, or to their neutralization by opposition of one against the other?
- As to the transmission to the horse of forces "emanating" from the rider, how can it work without the second having a point of support outside of the first...? Where then can the rider find this point of support?
- And of what constitutes so exactly this "appreciation" by the horse of the forces that are transmitted to him?

---

18   Professor of Hippology at the École de Cavalerie.

It was not easy to respond to so many questions with clarity while conserving the absolute value of the terms of the formula.

In truth, even if at the very beginning Baucher employed these terms to formulate his principle, and even if he persisted sometimes in using them in the heat of his oral teaching, as it appears probable from the works of his students, one must acknowledge that they are found only rarely in the text of his works, and only in the oldest by date (of publishing).

From 1842 onwards, in the thick of the dispute with his adversaries, the principle was already expressed with much less rigor, and with time, little by little it took on less and less radical forms. The instinctive forces, instead of being "destroyed," were to be "annulled," then "reduced," then "combated," and finally only "harmonized."

Expressed this way, the principle markedly moved away from the meaning that one could have given its first for the situation was that Baucher, as he so loved to do, had spoken with imagery, and forced the expression of his thoughts in order to make them more striking. With the first formula of his principle having remained the one most known, it is necessary to interpret it so as not to leave any equivocation. The deep study of his works, joined with long practice of his method, allows one to proceed without too much imprudence in this adaptation, and to bring the formula to an expression in which the meaning would probably be very close to this:

> "To eliminate all initiative by the horse in the use of his forces, with only the rider determining and regulating this use, solely in the measure and form decide by the rider, without according the least to the horse neither in the production nor in the mode of his activity."

The principle from the Old School was completely different.[19] On the contrary, it consisted of operating using horse's <u>natural instincts</u>.

---

19   Its *écuyers* were wary of establishing a formula. They wisely contented themselves with making discrete allusions in the exposé

Naturally inclined to dispense his "motor power" from behind forward, the horse was carefully and at length confirmed in this innate disposition. All other exercises that could possibly dissuade the horse were systematically avoided in his preliminary training.

Finally, with the horse's forces having been so to say "captured" by this preparation in a single direction, the *écuyer* endeavored to govern, regulate, and direct their output.

The Old School willingly consented to a certain loss of these forces, of which the instinctive expenditure could exceed the necessary; it preferred a prodigious horse to a parsimonious one, and accommodated a permanent excess of impulsion.

Instead of the participation liberally granted by a generous and willing helper, Baucher claimed to ensure the services of a conscientious provider, always ready "to Honour" received commands in quality as well as in quantity – but without a gram of extra effort. In summation, his new formula comes back to that of Talleyrand for his agents. "... and above all, no zeal!" (*Translator's note: Talleyrand was a French diplomat that worked successfully through the reign of Louis XVI to the French Revolution; known for polarizing opinions.*)

The Old School horse in his submission remained haunted by the fixed idea of forward movement. A Baucher horse had no other concern than to strictly conform to received orders, whatever their demand or direction, without ever anticipating them, nor, above all, exceeding them. The first remains "ambitious." The second risks becoming "indifferent." Baucher's detractors said, "That is no more than a resigned horse."

---

of their precepts, and we do not find it except from the pen of Comte d'Aure, who at the same time did not have any right to claim to be the faithful interpreter of his predecessors. The most typical form that the Comte d'Aure gave to this enunciation is in the following, "the best preparation for training a young horse is to habituate him to carry himself forward while pulling on his bridoon." (*Observations sur la Nouvelle Méthode d'équitation* (Observations on the New Method of Equitation))

The new principle necessarily had to bring about profound modifications in the practice of Equestrian Art. The subjugation of the horse became much stricter. The *"micrometric"* regulation of the expenditure of his forces and the mode of their use brought an exactitude and accuracy to his movements that the Old School had not known.

It was this precision that permitted Baucher and his pupils to approach and resolve equestrian difficulties that their predecessors had not envisioned, like changes of lead at every stride in the canter,[20] or the trot and canter backwards, and easily executed marked and repeated changes of direction in the work on two tracks for example, exercises that General l'Hotte tells us, "were not in the manner of the Old Masters."

One can however advance the notion, with some reason, that thirty-one new airs made possible by the application of Baucher's principle do not present any other interest than that of the difficulty conquered, that many of them deviated gracelessly from the majestic simplicity of the pure Art, and that the greater part of them were far from among the most gracious of *Haute École*.

The German *écuyers* were the most incredulous, and they declared that these airs could only have worked for Baucher by "trickery."

When the Berlin *écuyers* saw Baucher with their own eyes executing the changes of lead *au temps*, they masked their defeat by declaring – not without some reason – that this pretend air was in reality just a new artificial gait – and a defective one, according to them: a sort of "canter amble." (Seeger).

On the other hand, the increase in the horse's receptive sensibility to rider's indications demanded from the rider a corresponding increase in his skill in the use of his aids, in the dosage

---

20 When Baucher claimed that his horses could change lead at each stride of the canter, the Old School *écuyers* from all countries shrugged their shoulders. It seems for that matter that none of them had even tried anything like it in any era. The repeated changes of lead did not enter into their practice.

of their action, and the appropriate application. Absorbed by this constant preoccupation, the rider risks losing the ease of his position, by letting, as for example did Baucher himself, his head take a tilted attitude that the Master's admirers qualified as "meditative" and his detractors as "mournful."

The necessity to determine the production of the horse's energy at each moment brings the impulsive aids to such a disgraceful position of *"jambes plaquées,"* ridiculed in the caricatures that Lorentz made of the Master.

The minute tuning of the distribution of "transmitted" forces leads the hand to continual variations in its indications, up to provoking the uninterrupted *"pianotage"* that scandalized the Prussian *écuyer* so much when Baucher gave his performances with the Cirque Dejean in Berlin. Therefore it was not only because of his physical imperfections that Baucher lacked the presence of a "Nestier"[21], and that his position was so far from the "majesty" of a Franconi: The demands of the application of his method were not, without a doubt, completely irrelevant.

When all is said and done, despite some risks, from which the good students of Baucher knew how to escape, the new principle brought to the *Écuyer* an incontestable increase in power, and brought to artistic equitation an important enlargement of its domain.

For the "utilitarian" rider, and for the equitation that they practice, the value of this principle was far from being as high, without being negligible.

The outdoor rider indeed would not accommodate to the perpetual tension of the mind and body required by the full application of Baucher's formula; but judiciously restrained, sagely moderated, and opportunistically practiced the application of the formula could furnish him with powerful means for domination of difficult or defective horses, and also rapid means for the rudimentary education that would be sufficient for the service horse.

---

21   M. de Nestier, *écuyer* of Louis XV, model of academic equitation

It is this "tempered" application of the new principles that has been the object of the quest by all of Baucher's students who have been concerned with making his method applicable to everyday equitation.

"You would think that the man and the horse were but one," said Marquis de Dampierre of Monsieur de Nestier, model of academic equitation, and écuyer to Louis XV. One of the best horsemen in all of France; here training Louis XV's Florido. One may note the very short shanks of the curb bit, said to be "a la Nestier."

CHAPTER V - THE PROCEDURES

The fundamental procedure of Baucher's method, the one that applies directly to the first goal of his formula: to annul the instinctive forces, is the *"effet d'ensemble."*

It consists of the simultaneous use of the propulsive and the retraining aids in such a manner that the opposition of the forces, of which the aids determine the production in opposite directions, leads to the complete annulment of the forces. So, pushed forward by the legs, *tiré*[22] to the rear by the hands the horse has to stay completely immobilized by the *effet d'ensemble*.

This opposition must be made gradually. The forces deployed by the rider, "always equivalent," must be from the beginning as reduced as necessary to avoid any disorder. Little by little, the rider intensifies them to finally bring them up to the maximum of their potency; with the immobility of the horse remaining fully maintained if he is at the halt, and his gait remaining without modification if he is in movement.

Before seeking this equilibration of opposing forces, Baucher prepared for it by proceeding, separately for the forehand and the hindquarters, to the tuning and development of the power of the upper and lower aids.

By the adjustment of the direction of the aids, he made sure of the means to prohibit the horse from any disposition of his body susceptible to deviation from their directly opposed directions, the forces that must be neutralized by that opposition.

---

22 Put in a position. 'approaching the torso with the bridle hand.'

With the development of these aids, he carried the power of the *effet d'ensemble* to the limit. By putting into play the forces of the horse, demanded up to their limit, he made the horse feel, by containing those forces, the eventual futility of his efforts to escape from the constraint of the aids. The absolute domination of his instinctive forces, and by that, of his will, is thus realized. The horse, according to Baucher's expression is "bound in all four feet." Convinced of his helplessness, he is "tamed" and the effect "of the whole" is similar therefore to those systems of constraint invented with the same goal, from the twitch to the Barnum longe, passing by way of the pillars, the farrier's restraint, the Rarey system, and Raabe's Hippo-lasso.

The procedures for preparing for the *effet d'ensemble* are principally the "flexions" of the forehand and of the hindquarters. The two sets of flexions have the common goal of assuring the rider the means for moving the forehand and the hindquarters, each of them, in exactly the direction and position that he intends to give them.

By the imposition of thrusts rigorously fixed in their opposite directions, any possibility of "flight" of the forces by way of deviation is rejected. By the imposition of the position, which conditions the intensity of the effort (of the thrusts), the intensity can be brought to a degree corresponding to the imposed position.

In the forehand, it is by the shortening of the lever arm formed by the neck, the curling back of it on the trunk, and its "coiling" back on itself, which causes the moving back of the centre of gravity, slowing the progression of the body forward when it is pushed by the effort of the hindquarters.

This is the result sought in the "direct flexion" that leads to the *ramener*, where the action of the reins, with the normal position of the hand, finds advantage in acting perpendicularly to the bars, and, consequently, with great efficacy.

The lateral flexions have the essential goal of assuring the physiologic straightness of the neck by furnishing the means to combat any shifting of the neck to the side by bending it in the opposite direction. Consequently, these flexions contribute to stretching the muscles that oppose the *ramener*, and in addition prepare the direct flexion.

In his jaw the horse still possesses a centre of resistance to the constraint of the hand, whatever would be the position of his neck as he uses it, for example when diving onto the bit. The reduction of this aptitude for resistance is the object of the "flexion of the jaw," which compels the jaw to yield by opening under the pressure of the bit so that the tongue is mobilized up to its attachment under the poll, the relaxation of which is thus increased to further facilitate the direct flexion.

In the progression of these three essential flexions, that of the *ramener* is necessarily the last since its success depends in part on the results of the other two.

Adversaries to the "flexed" system would say: the dislocated, dis-articulated neck can no longer escape the *ramener* nor can the jaw escape relaxation. Together they constitute a shock absorber of the propulsion, adjustable at will, and of which the power of braking can be developed up to completely blocking the forward thrust of the *ressorts* of the hindquarters.

But Baucher was not content to have made the hand an un-crossable barrier, he wanted further to assure himself the power of coiling back the neck, a power capable of shifting the mass of the body from front to rear, and he wanted to impose continuity in its backward displacement.

He accomplished this by the exercise of *rein back*, but he would however only proceed after the lateral mobilization of the haunches that facilitates on one hand their later movement backwards and on the other hand permits interdicting their escape to the side.

For the hindquarters, the flexions consist of rotations of the croup around the shoulders, which makes the rider capable of moving as he wishes the former in relation to the latter in such a manner that it (the croup) would be constrained to dispense its effort exactly in the direction of the latter (the shoulders).

These rotations therefore play the role for the hindquarters that lateral flexion does for the forehand.

In a way, the direct flexion of the neck corresponds to the rein back for the haunches, one of the effects of which is to augment the effort of the closure of the articulations of the hindquarters, and thus to provoke an increase in the compression of its *ressorts*, the thrust of which regulate the intensity of the impulsion.

The comparison of these two preparations of the forehand and the hindquarters brings out a certain correspondence between them, which should lead to an equivalent development of the forces afterward destined to be counterbalanced in the *effet d'ensemble*.

Now, by the effect of lateral flexions applied to the forehand, just as to the hindquarters, this equivalence in the results of their preparation can well be considered realized insofar as it concerns the means of correcting the deviations of forces, but the equivalency stops there, and it is far from the same as it concerns the development of these forces.

After shifting the centre of gravity to the rear as a result of the *ramener*, the hand receives from the rein back a decisive back and forth power. Nothing analogous is effectuated in the reverse direction in the preparation of the hindquarters. No exercise is practiced to develop the intensity of the forward thrust of the hindquarters and to procure a propulsive power for the legs equal to the retro-pulsive power assured to the hand.

By the flexions of the rein back, the hindquarters have been *mise en mesure*[23] but not "on notice" to augment their propulsive effort.

---

23 This inequality between the preparation of the forehand and that of the hindquarters has preoccupied many of Baucher's students, including the best. Gerhardt recommended for remedying this inequality, "the frequent use of lively gaits," and of "rapid departs on the attack of the spurs." The Comte Alexis d'Abzac recommended, "give a good canter" to the horse immediately after the flexions. One

In the method, no exercise of "flight in front of the legs" corresponds to the "flight behind the hand" imposed by the rein back.[24]

"When the rider applies both legs, if their simple contact does not produce or re-establish the desired action, he touches the horse immediately with both spurs at the same time, without any opposition by the hand.

"The equivalence of forces" so quickly recommended by Baucher in the application of the *effet d'ensemble*, risks therefore being unable to be entirely realized in their opposition, and the difference in their intensities could only be produced to the detriment of impulsion.

It is one of the stumbling blocks of the method, and many of Baucher's students failed to avoid it. The forces developed by the hand, traction or resistances to traction, are too different in nature from forces developed by the legs, pressure or drumming, for the rider to be able to find in himself way of measuring the combined mechanical power. It is therefore their effects on the horse that he must be able to judge for their equivalence. Could he perceive that his mount comes to obey the indications of the hand willingly, but to obey those of the legs with reticence, all while appearing submissive to their presumably equivalent indications? Under Baucher's eye, yes, probably, thanks to the alert given by the Master, but if the student is reduced to only his own means, the trick risks escaping him. Submitting to the domination of the *effet d'ensemble*, the horse certainly renounces any effort *against* his rider, but his efforts *for* the rider risk lacking frankness.

---

finds nothing comparable in Baucher's works, except only in his "last teachings":
"When one applies the two legs, if their mere contact with the horse's sides does not immediately restore the desired action, one must right away touch with both spurs at once, without opposition of the hand.
He repeats these little attacks of the spur until the desired result is achieved... "The rider comes, by this means, to give the horse a great finesse to the leg...."
"Finesse" without a doubt, but power ?

24 *légèreté*

As soon as the submission of the *effet d'ensemble* at the halt is going well, Baucher undertakes the work in forward movement.

The essential thing for Baucher is that his student never deviates from the *ramener* accompanied by the mobility of the jaw, together constituting the *"mise en main."* As soon as "lightness[25]," characterized for Baucher by this *mise en main*, is changed, it must be re-established without delay by the *effet d'ensemble*, applied at first without interruption of the gait, then in place at a halt, imposed on the horse if the resistance persists, and is sustained until the horse has yielded, before a new depart.

This succession of departs and halts, necessarily close together in the beginning evidently can only be started at a walk sufficiently slowed down so that the alternating of movement and immobility can be carried out smoothly. It is thus that the walk becomes "the mother of gaits" for Baucher, instead of the trot, to which the Old Masters attributed this quality. His horse is exercised in the walk in all changes of direction, all the way to very tight turns, and worked on both one and two tracks.

When lightness is confirmed at the walk, the work at the trot is begun in the same conditions of slow measure as for the walk, and transitions between the walk and trot are practiced.

Then Baucher initiates the study of *"rassembler,"* for him intended to increase the mobility of the horse in all directions by the reduction of his base of support.

Submissive down to his skeleton to the demands of the aids, the horse, prepared by the flexions, confirmed in his lightness in place and in movement, pushed forward by the legs and held by the hand, brings his hind legs up closer to his forelegs, which is for the author of the method, the essential of the *rassembler* (13e Édition, p. 160).[26]

---

[25] One must observe that this concept of *rassembler* differs notably from that of the Old School (See Chapter: The Results).

[26] It is quite difficult not to attribute to General Faverot de Kerbrech, Editor of these "Teachings," a personal part in the clarification, so much later on, of a point in the method left obscured for forty years. (See Faverot de Kerbrech, *Methodical Dressage of the Riding Horse ...*, Xenophon Press 2010.)

It remains for the rider to animate his horse in this position in order to make use of the position, and this is another stumbling block on which the students of the Master came to hurt themselves.

It is quite evident that the effects of the hand and legs cannot be the same in the *effet d'ensemble* and the *rassembler* since, in the first case, they act to immobilize him, and in the second, to mobilize him, but one searches in vain, in the first twelve editions of the method, for a clear and precise explanation of the difference that surely must exist between them. It was only in Baucher's "testament," his "Last Teachings" appearing nearly twenty years after his death, that this essential distinction was clearly exposed with all the precision necessary[27]. In the *effet d'ensemble*, the legs proceed by continued and persistent action, by pressure; in the *rassembler*, their actions are brief and intermittent, there are repeated attacks. An analogous difference exists in the action of the hand in the two cases: while they are continuous for the *effet d'ensemble*, they are intermittent for the *rassembler*. What is more, the hand that "holds back" in the *effet d'ensemble* only "contains" in the *rassembler*.

It is beyond doubt that in his oral teaching, Baucher explained this difference to his students luminously. But they must have been somewhat perplexed later in reviewing the lesson, which had been received in the *manège*. The Master's books in numerous editions repeatedly said (up until the 13th edition) that the "immobility" of the horse actually achieved in the *effet d'ensemble* must remain complete under the most energetic attacks.

It was probably a slip of the pen, but it must have created plenty of trouble in the minds of his students.

Properly understood "mentally," this difference presented yet more serious difficulties in its application, because the agility of the hand certainly allows it to differentiate traction from

---

27 No difference in *placement* of the action of the legs between the *effet d'ensemble* and the *rassembler* was indicated by Baucher. It was Raabe, his student, who prescribed the application of the heels at the girth for the *effet d'ensemble* and behind the girth, on the flanks, for impulsion and the *rassembler*.

passive resistance so that it can easily regulate the intermittence of its actions, but the agility of the legs, exercised the same way, is much less, and the accord between the hand and legs is not always easy to regulate.

What is more, the horse trained from the beginning to the *effet d'ensemble*, and for a long time as a result rewarded for his immobility under the action of the legs, only wants, if he is cold, to make a mistake to the benefit of his rest upon feeling their action, and Baucher himself had that difficult experience, as General l'Hotte tells us (*'Un Officier de Cavalerie, Le Cheval Baucherisé'* en 1849 pages 109, 110, 111) ('A Cavalry Officer, The Baucherised Horse' in 1849),

"... Willingness in impulsion was difficult to obtain...

"... The horse finished by being blasé, hardened to the spur...

"... To relieve his legs, Baucher went to the whip... by repeated whacks, applied with more or less force..."

Seeger, from his side, wrote in 1852, after the performances of the Cirque Dejean in Berlin:

"The whip appeared to be a necessary instrument for M. Baucher. We never saw him without it, or riding the horse without using it... Monsieur Baucher used it with an extraordinary severity."

If Baucher himself experienced such difficulties in reviving impulsion numbed by the *effet d'ensemble*, what must have his students encountered trying to do so? It is not surprising that many of them were not able to succeed.

With a hot horse, there was less risk because it did not compromise the impulsion directly, but the confusion ran in the opposite direction: Put back into the *effet d'ensemble* after the study of the *rassembler*, the horse "forgot" the immobility previously obtained and substituted the mobility that had subsequently been taught in the *rassembler*. Most of the time, succeeding in preventing the horse from moving, if not creating piaffe: The domination was compromised.

"Kneaded" by the flexions, dominated by the *effet d'ensemble*, made mobile in every direction to the highest degree by the *rassembler*, the Baucher horse was ready to execute, on the weakest indication, all the movements that his neuro-motor organism allowed, even those least used in his normal activity.

It was sufficient, following the expression of the Master, to impose on the horse the "position" that allowed the movement and the "action" that determined the execution. After that, practice created habit, second nature.

These results of the method call for study, which is the object of one of the following chapters.

In its continuous evolution, explained below, the method conserved the greater part of his fundamental procedures, without modifying them radically.

Some of these procedures however have been subjected to some alterations profound enough to make one believe in their complete transformation, and even in their "reversal" if one could call it so. In reality, they have only been reworked in view of their particular accommodation to new arrangements of the methodical progression.

It is in the order of succession of these procedures that the evolution is the most visible. However, it is quite difficult to specify exactly the time when in the oral teaching of the Master, frequently digressing from his written teaching, this order of succession became exactly that which the sketch traced above has presented.

It was certainly part of the period when Baucher worked in the Circus (1838 – 1855). This era was subsequent to the first trials of the method in the Army (1842). The memoirs of General l'Hotte, who took his first lessons from Baucher in 1849, allow us to situate it around 1850.

Caricature by Lorentz
(in the "Musée Philipon")

CHAPTER VI - THE RESULTS

The results that Baucher obtained were extraordinary from all points of view.

It seems however that it would be the rapidity with which he obtained these results that should be raised first because it was nearly prodigious.

Two examples remain classic: Géricault, the Thoroughbred colt known by all of Paris for his rebelliousness and the violence with which he got rid of the most solid riders in the capital, including the Vicomte de Touron, champion of the d'Aurists, presented at the Circus by Baucher after 29 (or the 27th) days of training.

"The work that Baucher made him do that day," said General l'Hotte,[28] "was assuredly simple. It was also short, but absolutely correct... what would be marvelous," added the General, "would be to ride a similar horse, under the lights, to the noise of an orchestra and the applause of a large crowd, without his manifesting the least desire to defend himself, without even making one mistake."

Kleber, a nag with no capability, but an inveterate rearer, destined for the butcher for his rebelliousness, was also presented at the circus after a month of training.

These two tours de force were accomplished following challenges or bets. They had assuredly, before all else, a goal of demonstration and propaganda for the method. It must have been recognized, even among the most malevolent, that

---

28 It seems that General l'Hotte speaks here from hearsay, because he declares that he saw Baucher for the first time in 1849, and the presentation of Géricault was many years before that date.

the means of domination used by Baucher were of a power unequaled until that time.

It does not seem that Baucher suffered the least failure in this subject, nor was he even put into serious difficulty with any of the innumerable horses that he rode.[29]

The conditions under which he did his training, in the circus or in a public *manège*, would not have permitted any failure to be concealed and remain unknown in the state of overexcitement to which the intensity of Ptolemics had brought the world of riders, both partisans and adversaries of the new method. No failure by Baucher has ever been reported at any time in his career.

What is most remarkable yet is the persistence of submission in horses tamed by Baucher in this way. A declared partisan for Comte d'Aure, the Baron d'Étreillis himself pointed it out about Géricault:

"After having brilliantly contributed to the glory of his Master," he wrote, "Géricault was sold to Monsieur de Maucousin, an ordinary everyday rider, who used him for many years in sight of and recognized by all of Paris."

Kleber was ridden for many years at the circus by two écuyères, students of Baucher, Pauline Cuzent and Mathilde d'Embrun. He did not rear anymore, except on command for so-called courbettes.

Baucher's results were nonetheless remarkable for the development and variety that they allowed him to bring to the work of his horses.

At the canter particularly, the work constituted a veritable revolution in Equestrian Art.

The seated position of the horses of the Old School, by the surcharge that it imposed on their hindquarters, reduced the

---

29 The claim of Baucher's lack of solidity in the saddle appears quite difficult to reconcile with the constancy of victory that could hardly have been produced without some fights. In another instance General l'Hotte absolutely contests the insufficiency of his master's seat.

necessary mobility of the hindquarters for the instantaneous change in the canter. The lateral *placer* (position) systematically imposed on the horse at the canter necessitated a complete reversal of the *pli* for the execution of the change of lead. This operation consequently required too much time to allow any rapid succession of changes.

Also, frequent changes in the canter "had not entered the system of the old *écuyers*," General l'Hotte tells us. On the contrary, the Baucher horse, put into a "horizontal balance" according to his expression, that is to say equally weighted in front and behind, gained therefore an equal mobility of both the fore and hind of the diagonal pairs.

Moreover, kept constantly straight, without any lateral flexion to the side of the canter lead, he needed no change of *placer* to pass from one lead to the other, so well that the alternation of the leads, even at a single stride for each lead, became one of the daily exercises in his work, and one of the more characteristic among the new airs invented by the Master.[30]

It was again thanks to the horizontal balance of his horses, and the equal mobility in all directions that resulted from it, that Baucher could present his airs that were incontestably new, like the movement to the rear in trot, canter, and passage, the balancing of the haunches and of the shoulders,[31] the alternate movement forward and back on the same diagonal with the other diagonal remaining in support, or movements in place, etc.

---

30   In our time, when the changes of lead au temps have become one of the airs practiced regularly in School Equitation and now figure in the programs of international Grand Prix tests that often bring together thirty competitors, it is difficult to imagine the explosion of irony provoked by Baucher's pretension in making his horses change lead on each stride of the canter. In Paris, they had to rapidly recognize that this pretension was rigorously justified, but outside of France, above all in Germany, where the old equitation was still flourishing, the *écuyers* declared that it could only have been a "trick."

31   The balancing of the forehand in the piaffe was practiced in Italy, from where is given the name "Neopolitan Piaffe," to this air when it comported the balancing of the shoulders. (Translator's note: balancing is continuously making one step to the side alternatively on

The alternating elevation of the forelegs, in flexion or extension, seems to have been practiced in the circus before Baucher, but only in the work at liberty with the horse not ridden. The *jambette* obtained from the saddle on only the rider's aids could therefore also be considered a Baucher invention, as well as all the airs that derive from it, the walk called "Spanish" both forward and to the rear, Spanish trot, halts, pirouettes, and canter on three legs, etc....

Most of these new airs lent themselves to numerous combinations, to rapidly connected successions that gave the Master's horses' work a variety and brilliance completely unknown before him.

One could with good reason refuse to acknowledge in these "inventions" a classic character as it was understood before Baucher. One could contest their grace. But it is impossible to deny their inventor the merit of a difficulty conquered, and a power in the domination of a horse – the exploitation of his horses' capabilities, infinitely superior to that of all his predecessors.

As to the artistic value of Baucher's performances, with full knowledge of the facts, it is still somewhat difficult to judge.

It was "irreproachably correct," "dazzling," General l'Hotte tells us, and his admiration is assuredly a guarantee, the value of which could not be too highly appreciated. However, this admiration was not expressed without his adding some reservations, at least as it concerns "the Baucherised horse in 1849,"[32] and it is consequently appropriate to examine more closely the conditions in which this judgment was pronounced and formulated.

---

each side by either the forelegs, "balancing the shoulders" or the hind legs, "balancing the hindquarters.")

[32] See *Questions Équestres*, p. 111 (*Equestrian Questions*, see Hilda Nelson, *Alexis-François l'Hotte*, The Quest for Lightness in Equitation, J. A. Allen, London, 1997.)

In 1849, the method was sixteen years old, admitting that it dated only from the publication of *"Dictionnaire d'équitation"* (Dictionary of Equitation) in 1833. Baucher, who was more than fifty, had given performances at the circus for eleven years. He was in full possession of his mastery, and his reputation was solidly established.

His reputation does not appear to have subsequently declined in France, but it does not seem either to have been still growing. Outside of France, where it was much more discussed, it was in 1852 that it received its harshest criticisms. It seems therefore that one would be right to consider the "horse of 1849" as Baucher's "average" dressage horse *(cheval de dressage)* over the course of his career, because even if the method subsequently never stopped being modified, after the accident that Baucher suffered in 1855, School equitation *(equitation de dressage)* ceased to be the primary goal of his studies that, from then on, more and more envisaged the application of the method to everyday equitation.

On the other hand, in 1849, when he saw Baucher for the first time, Lieutenant l'Hotte was 24 years old. His equestrian experience was still very thin.

He had ridden a bit at his parents' home, but not at all at St-Cyr, done his course as *Sous-Lieutenant* at Saumur, and spent 3 years in his regiment. As an element of comparison that might have been able to serve as the base for his judgment, one can count little but the *Écuyer en Chef* at Saumur, Commandant de Novital, an enthusiastic disciple of the new method.

The young officer therefore could have been "dazzled" easily enough, but we must take count of the fact that in all likelihood his judgment only received its definitive editing more than thirty years later, and that the General elaborated at length on the keenness of the impressions of youth and the errors that it could provoke. One must think then that he carefully revised his own errors, if he committed some, and take to be entirely valid the judgment that he expressed in the following terms:

"The means put to use, clasping the horse in the embrace of the aids, had the consequence of holding him constantly contained and drawing his legs close together. The artificial balance that resulted made the horse essentially trained to concentrated lofty movements, where the horse must come back on himself, those for example like the following: piaffe, passage, pirouettes at the canter, changes of lead close together. But the horse was not in a situation to chase his body forward with ease and willingness. The rider, it is true, carried nothing in his arms, but he carried his horse in his legs." (General l'Hotte. *Un Officier de Cavalerie*, p. 111. (*A Cavalry Officer*))

In the public, a very large majority of admirers celebrated the success of the Master with a really delirious enthusiasm, but the "competent ones" on the other hand were almost all lined up on the side of his detractors.

These competent ones were otherwise of little number, and often of limited range because aristocratic equitation had died in France in 1830 with the School at Versailles.[33]

Nevertheless, it was to this School that had belonged, closely or loosely, nearly all the riders who could reasonably pretend to bring decent judgment to Baucher's work.

The two d'Abzacs were dead. At the death of the Vicomte d'Abzac, the premier *Écuyer* to Charles X had been forced to write, "... the service of the *Manège*, where Monsieur d'Aure is found to actually be the only man of a genuine talent...." And the talent of Comte d'Aure himself, as it concerned *Haute École* (High School dressage), was thin.

General l'Hotte acknowledged the statement without ambivalence. Describing the last demonstration of "Cerf," d'Aure's school horse at Versailles, he recognized it to have been only "complicated and without halts... composed of correct and counter leads and finished by changes of lead at each stride."[34] At Saumur, d'Aure's School horse, Neron, "also finished his

---

33 It had reestablished only a precarious existence from 1816 to 1830, because the second School of Versailles, reconstituted with difficulty, was never but a shadow of its great predecessor.

34 Which shows, parenthetically, how much d'Aure was, even at Versailles, already far from tradition, which did not comport any execution of changes of lead close together.

presentation by changes of lead close together.... It was neither by the regularity nor the elevation of his passage that he shone." – and General l'Hotte, after this reserved commentary we are left not knowing how in fact d'Aure was brilliant....

So d'Aure, eminent improviser, rider and trainer for the outdoors without equal, "the only man of a real talent" in the whole staff at Versailles was only of modest ability in *Haute École* and one must admit that his competence in the matter rests on limited fact.[35]

Almost all of the Masters of the *Manège* de Paris and their *Écuyers* came directly or indirectly, from the junior ranks of Versailles. Among the more aged riders, some had been attached in their youth to one of the two *Écuries* (*La Grande* and *La Petite*) as *élèves-piqueurs* (professional working students.) Others had received training, inevitably very elementary, given by former dabblers from Versailles at *"l'École d'instruction des troupes à cheval"* (Training School of the troops on horseback) or at *"l'École Nationale d'Équitation,"* formed successively after 1796 from the debris of personnel and material from the two *Écuries*. The younger of them, finally, had been *élèves-piqueurs* at the *Manège* reconstituted in 1816, and their number hardly passed a dozen. All of them claimed to be from Versailles, but very few of them possessed sufficient equestrian education to judge Baucher's work.

As to the *élèves-écuyers* of the Restoration, they were also few and none of them came to notoriety for their talent.[36] That was because the title of *Écuyer* was held by many charges of the Court who found their employment in equitation, but the title required no mastery.

---

35   It is appropriate to point out that, in his very sharp attacks against the new method, d'Aure wisely abstained from criticizing Baucher's talent for execution and the artistic value of his work. It was the absolute value of the method for the use of the horse outdoors that he contested.

36   Except for Lacosme-Brèves, but even if he was certainly a student at the *Manège des Pages*, it is not certain that he was really an *élève-écuyer* at the *Manège* de Versailles.

The students in the *"Manège des Pages"* that depended on Versailles for teachers totaled 318 from 1816 to 1830. They received good practical training but nothing more. Despite their three year course they only rode three times a week, "20 to 25 minutes a lesson." They were not competent to judge Baucher.[37]

In the cavalry, the equestrian practice was at a very low level. A great number of the older officers did not have any instruction on a horse other than the "classes" for recruits of the Empire, squeezed in between campaigns. The more favored had received a little less rudimentary but quite incomplete training at the *École de St-Germain*.

The young officers, of whom only a few went to the *Manège des Pages*, did indeed in great number pass through the *École de Cavalerie*, but the instruction that they received there left them with troubled minds for lack of uniformity in the teaching. In the military instruction, only the simple principles of Bohan were allowed. In the *manège*, the teaching claimed to remain academic, although there was a marked discord between the *Écuyer en Chef*, Monsieur Cordier, who claimed to represent Versailles, and his second in command, Monsieur de Chabannes, a declared partisan of the principles of d'Auvergne. Even after the departure of Monsieur de Chabannes, the principles of d'Auvergne remained the preference of Monsieur Rousselet who did not hide it and did not leave the school until 1848.

The *"Cours d'équitation"* (*Course in Equitation*), published in 1829, had officially and theoretically well re-established the unity of equestrian doctrine in the School. But it was not so in practice and the results of instruction were found to have gravely suffered when the conversion to Baucherism in 1842 by the *Écuyer en Chef*, Commandant de Novital, caused disarray in the training.

As factors of observation being able to serve as a base for appreciation of the work of the horses of Baucher that they all

---

37 Among the "competent ones" of the time, we should not forget Franconi, who certainly had no relation with Versailles. Venetian by birth, he had received his equestrian training in Italy. Franconi was on the other hand far from lining up with Baucher's detractors, however without ceasing to keep his own manner of riding and training.

went to see at the circus, the officers who followed courses at Saumur after 1842 could well admire "Ourphaly," Commandant de Novital's horse, but his example could not be put up in opposition to those of Baucher, since he was Baucher's student. It allowed them to observe the different degrees of perfection in the same training system. As to officers who had followed the courses before 1842, they still had role models in *Haute École*. The *Écuyer en Chef* from 1825 to 1834, Monsieur Cordier, was more a skilled equestrian artisan than an artist. He especially lacked presence and prestige.[38] Monsieur Rousselet had more presence. He excelled at getting the most out of difficult horses. His own horses' work was charming in its confident submission and gracious ease, but it remained very simple and could not serve as a base of comparison with the work of Baucher's horses.

It is therefore difficult to appreciate the artistic value of the performances of the Master based on the judgments of his French contemporaries. The crowd of his admirers was composed mostly of laymen, or of semi-connoisseurs. His rare detractors, among whom were almost all of the competent people of the era, aimed their criticisms particularly at the practical value of the new method more than at the results obtained by Baucher in the training of his horses.

Outside of France, especially in the Germanic countries, riding flourished. Over the Rhine, despite the upheavals of the revolutionary and Napoleonic period, equitation was far from having suffered the same eclipse as in France. The School at Vienna, the Versailles of central Europe, had never ceased to function as a conservatory of equestrian art and as a seminary for *écuyers* from all of Southern Germany. At Göttingen, the *Manège* at the University continued to flourish and attract not only riding youth from the Kingdom of Hanover, but numerous students from England, and even from France, in a rush to be taught by the celebrated Ayrer brothers. In Prussia, military

---

38 He had a belly and when he had the arches (part of the thigh blocks – see Command Licart, *Évolutions Équestres, à travers les ages*, Olivier Perrin Éditeur, Paris, 1963) on the front of the *Manège* saddles lowered, malicious Sous-Lieutenants claimed that it was because the *Écuyer en Chef* "had wounded himself in the belly button."

equitation was doubtlessly more cultivated than artistic equitation, but the training of army horses was pushed so far that the equestrian competence of the cavalry officers attained an elevated level. The top management of equestrian instruction for the army was entrusted to civilian *écuyers* of great esteem like Seeger and Seidler.

Baucher on Partisan: Piaffe

After 1815, the royal stables and the stables of the principalities had been reestablished in the numerous Courts of Germany, as well as the *manèges* that complemented them before the revolution, in Bavaria, at Wurtemberg in Saxony, in the Grand Duchy of Bad, etc.... Everywhere equestrian art had regained its sanctuaries and its homage flourished anew. By crossing the Rhine, Baucher went to find his judges.

During his early tours in Germany, the critics seemed reserved. They had been a little disconcerted by the novelty of the spectacle, speechless before the striking differences that separated the work of the innovator's horses from traditional equitation.

In the army, the new method attracted close attention. Many generals, like the Prince of Hohenlohe and the von Willisen brothers, studied it with care. Numerous officers of all ranks also took lessons from Baucher. The general impression was far from unfavorable, and some enthusiasts quickly and clearly took up the cause for the new method.

The civilian *écuyers* remained cautious. Seidler, who taught at the "Lehreskadron" in Berlin, an equestrian school for officers, profited from Baucher's return to Paris to go there and discreetly spend several weeks introducing himself to the practice of the new method.

But an intense reaction against this sudden fancy was not long in coming, and Seeger took the lead of the movement. No one could contest Seeger's competence, and everyone feared the cut of his claws, because he was aggressive, and acerbic.

Heir to the knowledge of an old family of *écuyers*, Seeger had studied his art for a long time at the School in Vienna under Max von Weyrother. He openly proclaimed his fidelity to the principles of the Old School and claimed to represent de la Guérinière, even though his personal practices were singularly far from those of that master. Seeger, who directed, under the protection of the Court, the largest *manège* in Berlin, had a very high opinion of his own worth and severely judged all of his colleagues. Seidler was particularly the object of his criticisms with no benevolence, and Seeger considered it a denial of justice that the equestrian direction of Lehreskadron had been entrusted to Seidler when Seeger thought himself to be the one solely worthy.

In 1852, Seeger published a harsh attack against the new method that he entitled "Serious Warning to the Riders of Germany." This work is the only document that contains a methodical examination and detailed criticism of the results obtained by Baucher, the subject of this chapter. It is advisable then to examine the content of this pamphlet with care.[39]

One should probably separate the observations of its author from the judgments that he pronounced. Seeger's equestrian knowledge and his long practice lead us to admitting the exacti-

---

39   See Appendix II

tude of the observations, especially since they often corroborate what we already know about Baucher's horses. But the terms applied to these observations might inspire some presumptions of excess in their measure.

As to the judgments that Seeger applied to his observations, one must take into account that they are always based on the hypothesis of the absolute value, permanent and intangible, of the "canons" of the Old School, considered as the one and true Church, whereas Baucher intended precisely to found a "reformed" church, a New School of which the "canons" were very different from those of the old one.

One must also consider the bilious character of Seeger, and his animosity toward Seidler, whom he pursued through Baucher.

The time in which Seeger's pamphlet was launched was particularly unfavorable to Baucher and to his German partisans. Seidler had completely failed in a trial application of the Baucher's method in Berlin. Seidler did not have enough modesty to admit that the superficial knowledge he had acquired in several lessons in Paris could have had its part in that failure. He preferred to attribute his lack of success to defects in the new method, which he renounced with so much zeal that the Court and the high authorities of the army joined the movement of reaction in favor of the Old School.

As for Baucher, he had committed some grave imprudence. In his last few seasons in Berlin, he had brought only horses of a second caliber. Many of these horses were ridden by two of his student *écuyères* (horsewomen.) Upon the horses' return to France they had been neglected in their work in the hands of these women. Baucher himself presented barely two newly trained horses, Blacknick and Rufus, who were far from being counted amongst the best of his career.

Blacknick had a *mauvais cœur* (bad temperament), so lazy that it was necessary to rudely animate him in the corridor before entry into the arena. As to Rufus, he was already worn out and had been stiff in his hindquarters before his training. He was long and weak in his top line, with a long-eared heavy head. His training had certainly been one of those tours de force in which Baucher excelled, but the horse remained an ungracious oaf that should never have appeared in public. He executed almost all of the work in which Partisan had been so brilliant, but "like a goose imitating a swan."

The basic criticisms formulated by Seeger on the work of Baucher's horses concerned their balance and their general attitude (*attitude d'ensemble.*) As for their balance, said Seeger, it remained – when all went well – horizontal, that is to say, appropriate at most for outdoor equitation. They were never on the haunches, and on the contrary frequently fell onto the shoulders.

As to their position or frame that Baucher unduly called "*rassembler*", it had of *rassembler* only the bringing together of the four feet. The systematic lowering of the neck unloaded the hindquarters and loaded the shoulders. Since the raising the neckline did not occur, the hindquarters failed to receive the necessary weighting operations required to cause their closure, therefore the upper joints of the hindquarters remained open, croup remained high, the back legs outstretched while the forehand was crushed by the entire weight of the horse's front end and that of the rider.

In this position, between the forehand and haunches, the top line lifts and the loins stiffen by arching. These horses were "under themselves" in front and behind. Their position was that "of a mountain goat with his four legs close together on the summit of a peak."

In his examination of the gaits, Seeger stressed the defects of the trot, in which the weight of the shoulders precipitated the fall of the forelegs to the ground, which they "seemed to leave with regret."

The School walk was unknown to these horses. Their passage, like their trot, lacked *tride* (liveliness). At the piaffe, the hind legs went wide as they came down to the ground and *se balancent lateralment* (balance themselves sideways) instead of flexing vertically, while the forelegs stamped without lifting the forehand, and the croup on the contrary hopped at each step.

At the canter, Baucher's horses "seesawed," lifting and lowering in turn the forehand and the hindquarters by a "movement analogous to that of waves."

The tempi changes visibly embarrassed Seeger who could not deny the reality of their execution. He got out of that by declaring that they constituted in reality a new artificial gait "similar to an amble."

Seeger also vividly criticized Baucher's riding procedures. According to Seeger, Baucher's horses threw themselves to the side in the turns, with the shoulders falling in the new direction for lack of being supported by the engagement of the hindquarters, particularly the inside hind leg.

It was the same in the work on two tracks where the inside hind due to lack of engagement and flexion was incapable of receiving and supporting the body which "rolls to the side."

In these conditions, the pirouettes could not be correct and were effectively nothing but "circular scrambles."

Finally, the rein back of Baucher's horses was nothing but a hurried hiding behind the bit, the pressure of which the horse refused.

With regard to the rider, Seeger was not less severe. Baucher constantly sat on his fork, his buttocks *"en porte-manteau,"* (a large suitcase with two hinged sections) his torso leaning forward, his head in a "weighed down" position. His legs remained invariably jammed onto the horse, and his spurs endlessly combing, all the way up to the sheath, the flanks made insensitive by the uninterrupted bite of the rowels. His right hand "pianoed" convulsively, sometimes on the bridoon reins, sometimes on the curb reins, when it was not occupied in cruelly whipping the hindquarters.

On these observations, Seeger formed and pronounced merciless judgments:

Baucher's work had no rapport with that of true *Haute École* that consists, above all, of the lightening of the forehand, obtained by the deep engagement of the hindquarters, lowered by the flexion of all of his articulations, especially those of the hip and stifle.

To request the School airs from a horse that is in a balance that hardly permits the easy use of natural gaits was a crime of *lèse-équitation*. The supposed airs that Baucher had the effrontery to present were nothing but a caricature of what they ought to be, and only ignorant people could allow themselves to be seduced by this shameful counterfeit. Baucher was not only a "charlatan," he was the "grave digger of French equitation."

It seemed that this pamphlet would remain totally unknown in France. Neither Baucher's enemies nor friends breathed a word about it. The latter would certainly not have failed to respond in no uncertain terms, and one must admit that they would have had the better part of the argument considering the exaggerations and evident preconceptions of the author.

It was not a portrait of Baucher's horses that Seeger drew; it was a caricature of Rufus! But as forced as may be the thrust of this charge, it followed the general contours of the model, and even the deformations that he made of it could only underscore, without evident indulgence, at least the potential defects that were often more or less accentuated.

In all likelihood, according to what we know, the results of the method would almost always present certain questionable characteristics, that were probably reduced to tendencies for the "successful" horses, but inevitably became more marked for the others.

Even taking into account the natural and overexcited malevolence of the bad tempered Seeger, one could still admit the well founded part of his observations. In comparison to the "portrait of the Baucherised horse" drawn by General l'Hotte, we can place the "caricature" of the same horse drawn by Seeger.

When he reproached Baucher's horses for being *rassemblé* only in their underline, one must recognize that the pictures of the new method and more yet, Adam's album, gave him reason to do so.

The shortening of their spinal column is not proportionate to their base of support. The flexions of the spine with all its curves that determine the shortening of the spine are limited to the neck. The two other curves that follow in the opposite direction from the withers to the back of the croup escapes Baucher to the point where the loins of his horses straighten instead of adding to the natural flexion and even tends to bend in the opposite direction creating an arch.

It is possible that the artists did not reproduce their models in complete fidelity, and Baucher was frequently in sorrow about that. However the distortions that they were able to represent were not at all inspired by malice, and they could hardly have done more than exaggerate tendencies to which we certainly must admit.

But when Seeger, after having reproached Baucher's horses for "rocking" at the canter, claims that his own – who of course are the models – do not rock and that their trunks keep a constant angle relative to the ground, higher in the withers than in the croup, we can affirm that he is mistaken, and that his horses rocked (basculed) just like Baucher's.

Even before the confirmation by moving pictures confirm it, the experiments by Lenoble du Teil destroyed the illusion so dear to Seeger and shared by many of the old *écuyers*. The horse always rocks (bascules) at the canter, the same at the *terre-à-terre*, the same at the *mézair*, because landing on the ground and suspension are produced in alternating order for the forehand and the hindquarters, the height of the forehand and croup above the ground can not remain equal during these two phases, and these variations are produced in alternating times for the withers and the croup.

In the diagonal gaits, it is quite probable that Seeger's horses, seated as they were, had more lightness in the forehand than Baucher's horses, but on the other hand, the Baucher's could extend more vigorously than could Seeger's whose horses' hind legs were suppressed by the weight of their hindquarters. The duration of suspension in all likelihood was more ample in Baucher's horses than that of Seeger's horses. There were necessarily very marked differences in the form of their two passages. Wasn't the passage that Baucher advocated more natural, true to his goal, and closer to the passage that the horizontal horse develops with such grace?

As for the criticized distortions in Rufus's piaffe, they likely resulted, just as for many others, from the difficulties of the trade to which Baucher was reduced. His contracts with the directors of the circus, as much with Dejean as with Soulier, obliged him to always have six horses, each having their "number," of which four must always be ready to "enter the ring." It is enough for one to have trained some school horses to be able to comprehend the impossibility of fulfilling the same conditions without having to "fake" the work for the performance.

To find, at an acceptable price, a horse presumed apt to furnish correct, if not brilliant, work is an arduous problem. Two disappointments in three purchases are standard. The training of these "specialists" is one of the more thankless tasks. The least accident, the most banal unavailability interrupts it, delays it, and often compromises it. For every successful dressage horse, incredible disappointments attend the artist regardless of his ability and the unrelenting work. In order to satisfy the demands of his impresario and to present only impeccable performances, Baucher required three times as many horses than the circus held for him in board.

And then, Baucher wanted to prove that with his method all horses could execute the work that was reserved by the Old School to subjects of its choice. He came inevitably to "stylize" not only the gaits, but also their defects, and even the unruly predispositions of his horses, and to present them as "variations" on classical airs.

Hence his son Henri tells us, that he "excelled even at taking advantage of their flaws." It was the natural stamping of "Stadiums" that was provoked the piaffe, discretely qualified as "precipitated." So it is quite probable that Rufus's wobbly hocks went for much in his piaffe *"balancé"* that scandalized Seeger.

And Baucher went yet farther. Exploiting among others Kleber's tendency to "point," he made his *écuyères* execute alleged *"courbettes,"* which were nothing but rears and leaps. Such fantasies could the very easily mislead the lay people of Paris, but it was foolhardy to try to impose the same movements suitable for Berlin.

As to the manner of executing turns, Baucher was perhaps not much more satisfied than Seeger. He wrote in 1842:

"Whatever lightness that my horse had on a straight line, I noticed that the lightness always lost delicacy on tight circles even though my outside leg came to the assistance to the inside. As soon as the hind leg put itself in movement to follow the shoulders on the circle, I immediately felt a slight resistance. I told myself to change my use of the aids and to apply the leg on the side opposite the turn. At the same time, instead of immediately carrying my hand to the right to direct the shoulders, I first created, with the aid of the hand, the opposition necessary to fix the haunches and direct the forces in a manner to maintain balance during the execution of the movement. This procedure was crowned with complete success."

One can not see very well what is the change in use of the outside leg, which at first, "came to the assistance of the inside leg," and "then was applied." Could it come to help "without being applied"? It seems therefore that the change brought to the use of the legs is only the suppression of that of the interior leg.

And was the success as complete as Baucher wrote? One could doubt it, since from 1864 on, at the dawn of the Second Manner, Baucher again completely changed the use of his aids for turning, to be obtained then by the sole pressure of the outside rein without the intervention of the legs – only to return ten years later in his last edition to "the eventual use" of the inside leg in view of "placing the haunches" and to second as needed the action of the outside rein.

Amongst these procedures, vastly different from one another and described successively by Baucher as "definitive," how much trial and error had to be experienced without giving satisfaction, even temporarily?

Couldn't it have been one of these intermediate periods that Seeger's observation recorded in 1852 applied?

As to the pamphleteer's (Seeger's) lampooning judgments based upon these observations, he pronounced them by application of the rules of aesthetic assuredly very old and respectable, but one that could claim neither sustainability nor universality. On the other hand, it was precisely a new aesthetic that Baucher intended to found. One could accept it or reject it, but it is not judicious to condemn his new canon by application of the old one.

For his predecessors, the supreme goal of artistic education of the horse was the "elevated airs" or "School jumps."[40] For Baucher, who deliberately neglected these airs "above the ground," the goal of *Haute École* was only the stylization of the natural gaits by the accentuation of their rhythm, and the development of the horse's agility in his normal movements.

The Old School *écuyer* had to achieve as complete a lightening of the forehand as possible in order to achieve his goals. In the pesade a horse must be able to maintain itself in the air with all of its weight resting on the hindquarters. Baucher had no use for a similar requirement. On the contrary, it would even go against his goals, it would clash with obtaining the results he sought and would be in contradiction with the rules of his new aesthetic that, although clearly different, was not inferior to the Old Masters.

General l'Hotte's judgment is therefore without any doubt better founded than that of Seeger. Seeger's judgment applies to mediocre or bad horses that Baucher had the necessity to present because of professional constraint. These horses probably merited some of Seeger's criticism and Baucher was certainly not ignorant of it.

General l'Hotte's admiration applies to the Master's "successful" horses: Partisan, Captaine, Neptune, Buridan, and such others. Their performances were certainly "irreproachably correct" and their artistic value "dazzling." It is by the Cid, and

---

40 From which comes their position of a "cat ready to jump onto the table" that Baucherists in derision attributed to them so as to reply in response to that of a "cat making his back big," attributed to Baucher's horses by his detractors.

by Horace, that one judges Corneille. Agésilas and Attila have not tarnished his glory.

As for the results obtained by Baucher's students, they were naturally very uneven.

Almost all who followed the Master's direct oral teaching for a sufficient peri od for it to penetrate, obtained satisfactory results, even if their previous equestrian instruction had not been developed. Those who already had been experienced and very gifted riders beforehand nearly always achieved a real talent. The most celebrated among them, General l'Hotte, perhaps surpassed his Master. Colonel Guérin, the Comte de Montigny, Captain Raabe, General de Kerbrech became masters in their turn. A great number of others became skilled *écuyers*. Many of them modified certain practices of the method to adapt it to particular goals and according to their own aptitudes,. But none of them rejected the method after having practiced it under the direction of its author.

It never worked the same for those who received the teaching of the new method "second hand," even when transmitted by Baucher's good students, probably because the didactic aptitude of the students was not at the same level as their skill in execution, nor certainly was it comparable to that of the Master.

As for the riders that attempted to apply the method only from Baucher's written teaching, one cannot cite anyone who succeeded even modestly. Almost all of them, even despite the previous equestrian experience of some, were forced to renounce their trials after painful disappointments. Rul, the most loyal among all of the disciples of the Master, deplored these renunciations in these terms:

"When one reflects that there is perhaps not in the world a single cavalry officer, a single amateur, that has not sought, *book in hand*, to apply this new method, one could imagine what kind of tower of Babel would come out of these countless attempts without a guide....

"It would take a book to write down the entire burlesque, ridiculous, against the grain applications that I have seen of the method. One rider has so confounded the functions of legs and hands that the horse backs up instead of going forward... and yet he has applied the Baucher method! Another has so lowered the neck that his horse resembles a truffle hunter more than man's beautiful conquest! 'Baucher's Method!' Another fan, fresh out of college, who believes himself a rider because he has twice used his 'twenty-four stamps' (tickets) for the *manège*, also wants to practice the Baucher Method. Oh! Surprise! His horse neither advances nor backs up, but turns in place with the rapidity of a Hindoustani pearl threader. 'Satanic Method!' A fourth has so unequally distributed his weight that his horse, instead of going straight, incessantly travels on a diagonal line. One could believe seeing one of these collegians measuring, with blindfolded eyes, the lawn at Versailles. '*E semper* the Baucher method!'"

After that, and while continuing to believe firmly that the artistic value of Baucher's work had been, as General l'Hotte affirmed, "dazzling," one could think that the clarity of his works had been a good deal less so.

CHAPTER VII - EXPERIMENTATION WITH THE METHOD IN THE ARMY

On 17 March 1842, Lt. General Oudinot addressed to Baucher the following letter:

"Monsieur,

"Following the propositions that you made to M. le *Maréchal*, Minister of War, His Excellency has decided that a series of experiments will be held in Paris to test your method for training remount horses, and horses that are recognized as difficult. Consequently, one hundred young horses taken from the Regiments of the Paris Garrison will be trained according to your method. The trials will take place in the presence of a Commission composed of Captain Instructors from the 5th *Cuirassiers* and the 3rd *Lancers*. The *Chef d'escadrons* commanding the *manège* at the Cavalry School, whom the Minister has ordered to Paris, will take part in this commission, of which the presidency has been confided to me. Before giving instructions to the *Maréchal de Camp* commanding the Brigade and to the Colonels of the two regiments, I need, Monsieur, to meet with you."

"I pray you, consequently, would be so kind as to come tomorrow at 9 o'clock to my home, where these gentlemen will meet us."

"Receive, I pray you Monsieur, the assurance of my greatest consideration.

Lieutenant General
Marquis Oudino"

The General was not just content with winning the Duc d'Orléans to Baucher's cause, he had even extensively prepared the conditions in which the agreed upon trials were going to take place, and assured himself of the support of the *Manège* at the Cavalry School, in which he knew better than anyone else the authority (vested) in the cadres of that army. At the beginning, he had obtained agreement from the Minister that Monsieur Rousselet, *Écuyer* at the School for more than 25 years and venerated by his students, would be sent to Paris to study the new method and become knowledgeable in its practices.

This visit did not produce a great result. The old *écuyer* did not contest the value of the demonstrations by Baucher, but he found himself disoriented on "Capitaine," the horse that the Master had offered him to ride and truthfully he was not able to ride the horse to his advantage. With his habitual reserve and modesty, he returned to Saumur very perplexed, and he refrained from pronouncing a definitive judgment on the new method. However, he could not be the firm support at the Cavalry School *Manège* that the General had wanted to assure to his protégé.

To overcome this semi-failure, the General obtained from the Minister the dispatch to Paris of the *Chef d'escadrons* commanding the *Manège*, Commandant Delherm de Novital, so that he in turn could study Baucher's method. Despite the hierarchy that gave him precedence over M. Rousselet, the authority of Commandant de Novital in matters of equitation was less than that of his subordinate, and on almost every equestrian subject, these two *écuyers* were in complete disagreement.

It was not different with regard to Baucher's new method. In listening to Baucher, Commandant de Novital was struck by a sudden illumination. The constraint imposed by Baucher on his horses, was so far from the systematic gentleness of M. Rousselet, entirely suited the manner of the *Écuyer en Chef*, who returned to Saumur converted to the new faith and determined, such a Polyeucte[41] to overturn the old idols.

---

41 (Ref: Roman martyr: Polyeucte)

The experiment, which was to begin the 21st of the same month, five days after the General's letter, was difficult to conduct well. The methods of instruction for the troop in use at military *manèges* would not permit it to work. Despite the prescriptions of the Ordinance of 1829 which had replaced that from the year XIII, instruction remained collective, that is to say the opposite of that given by Baucher. The Ordinance had certainly recommended "instruction in small groups" but the materiel difficulties and the persistence of routine had kept or brought back the practice of "classes" as numerous as were permitted by the rare *manèges* that arranged them. To give a lesson to recruits in the Cavalry School, the instructor, at attention as was his troop that was arranged in regular formation, was confined to reciting "in a commanding tone" the literal text of the Ordinance. Then the class, formed up on parade at a fixed distance behind a "trained rider," executed well or badly the commanded movement while following its guide.

The remarks had "to include, as much as possible, the repetition of textual requirements of those regulation prescriptions of which the instructor fell to failure." These remarks applied to only two points judged to be essential: the position of the riders and the conservation of the distances in the parade ranks. It was normal usage to add a few classical formulae, like "sit, sit!" or "fixed hand and legs close" that doubtlessly brought no great comfort to the distress of the recruits in perdition.

Over months, the movements executed were merely successive. When the individual movements were finally started, they had to be executed simultaneously by all the riders, and the rigorous observation of intervals then replaced that of the distances in the preoccupations of the instructor.

After eight months of this regime, the more resourceful of the young riders were recognized as "apt to pass on to the Squadron School." None of them had ever galloped or cantered alone outside.

In 1842, many superior officers had not received any other instruction on a horse. The young ones, at the Saumur *Manège* or at the one for the Pages, had received more personal and direct instruction, but still it was very far from the individual form that Baucher gave in his own instruction.[42]

The training of young horses in the Cavalry was no less collective than the instruction of the recruits. The instructors patiently routined each like the other, and for the horses, the extremely low level of grain rations quite easily allowed them to acquire a resignation that took hold instead of real training.

What is more, the instruction of recruits and the training of remounts were not done in the *Corps* of Troops, but at the depots,[43] where the personnel specializing in these two functions necessarily resided.

So, theoretically at least, Baucher's dressage lessons were not going to be applied to young horses mounted by trainers, but to horses already in service, mounted by their usual riders. Happily for him, it was not completely so. The shortage of

---

[42] It is quite difficult now to imagine the form of this instruction at Saumur, where the corrections applied to the position quite a lot more than to the use of the aides. One detail, not a little picturesque, can give us an idea. At each of the annual Inspections of the Cavalry School, the Commandant Major proposed the elimination of the costly *manège* hats, imposed on all the students for equestrian exercises for the complete duration of their courses, but that they could not use anymore afterwards.

The Major's proposition was invariably pushed back by the Inspector General, convinced of the necessity to keep this hat by the argument that the *Écuyer en Chef* opposed to its suppression:

"The *manège* hat is indispensable to allowing the *Écuyer* to easily see the defective positions of his students. The direction of its wings (Translator's note: the front of the brim was folded up against and around the crown with the back brim folded straight up to the crown and the remainder of the brim flat leaving observable straight wings) revealed immediately the defects in rectitude of the position of the man who wore it that risked passing unnoticed without this means of obvious and continuous control."

So they passed on, from promotion to promotion (class), these *manège* hats that were so elegant to wear, grease stained and worn threadbare, "completely impregnated with the sweat of the *anciens*."

[43] The regiments changed garrison at least every two years. They were frequently stationed many hundreds of kilometers from the depots that were, on the contrary, rarely moved.

horses in the Army was so great that, as much as possible, they avoided sending them to train at the depots after their purchase. All those that showed themselves a bit close to usable in the ranks were immediately assigned there. These were the greater number, because in France the purchasing officers found hardly a quarter of the effective strength that they were supposed to acquire annually. The rest came from outside of France.[44]

For lack of choice, they had to accept many horses that were "used," if not used up. At least they presented the advantage of being mostly usable. A regimental reserve of about fifteen horses, called the "Little Remount," was constituted in each *corps*, and placed under the direction of a Captain Instructor. It had the goal of allowing the squadrons to maintain an effective strength that was more or less equal, despite the frequent and sudden deficits caused by the bad state of health and the upkeep of the horses that left a lot to be desired.

At the "little remount," they placed, quite naturally, the least wise of the horses from among the "newcomers." The Captain Instructor with some petty officers and riders, completed their preparation albeit badly.

On the other hand, it was physically impossible for the Regiments in Paris to satisfy the demands of the grueling *service de la Place* and, at the same time, to furnish the one hundred horses required by the *Note de Service* from General Oudinot. At the meeting on 18 March, to which he had been summoned, Baucher accepted that the number of horses destined for the experiment would be reduced by three quarters. This way he would have the benefit of the satisfaction of the Colonels, and the power to practice his experiment at a reduced level. That alone would allow the individual application of his instruction procedures.

He went even further in his wise moderation, and proposed that only two horses from each regiment be brought to him on the first day, four the next day, and so on up to a maximum of 10 or 12 for each corps. His proposal was accepted with enthusiasm by the Colonels: by itself the "little remount" nearly sufficed to

---

44   In 1840 therefore, 34,000 horses were purchased outside of France, coming for the most from Germany and Hungary.

furnish the horses destined for the experiment without impoverishing the squadrons, already reduced to at least two thirds of their normal effective strength....

The experiment prescribed by the Minister was announced under the best auspices for the author of the new method. The arrangements for the Examination Commission, presided over by General Oudinot, were not in doubt, and its report would be written up by Commandant de Novital, who did not hide his enthusiastic attachment to the new school.

Baucher's skillful moderation, and his comprehension of the material difficulties of service, had entirely won to his cause the *Marechal de Camp* commanding the Paris Brigade and his two Colonels, who decided as a result to facilitate in all possible measure the execution of an experiment of which they had at first been doubtful.

Finally and above all, the new conditions in which it was going to take place were exactly those that Baucher considered to be the most favorable.[45]

He did not fail in any way to call upon all his skillful resources, and right away found a simple tone, without familiarity, that was appropriate to his new students' understanding without compromising the authority that he had to win and gain over them for lack of the rank conferred by the epaulette.

To the luminous clarity of the explanation of each of his precepts, he added the practical demonstration, on the spot, of the corresponding procedures, and put his finger on the nature and form of the result to be obtained. He then made each of the riders execute under his eye what he had just showed them himself. Directing with his own hand that of the student, or placing the student's leg at the favorable place, he made the student develop, measure, and direct his force, acting or resisting, imposing or opposing, and finally yielding as soon as the submission of the horse was achieved.

The riders showed themselves to be extremely attentive to Baucher's explanations, and a most lively competitive emulation

---

45   See Appendix I, Memoirs of E. Caron.

arose among the students from the first hour's lesson. They were pleased to figure as monitors, while the new students hurried to make up for their delay.

The Master wisely limited the application of his method to what was necessary for a troop horse and to the equestrian aptitude of the average rider, particularly in so far as it concerned the use of the spur.

The results were excellent, and the success of the experiment incontestable. On 3 April, after 26 sessions of training with two lessons a day, the horses maneuvered in all directions at the canter, or worked correctly on parade at the same gait, without getting out of hand, and without trying to avoid the hand. Similar results perhaps have not been without example in the most successful training conducted in the old manner, but they had only been obtained after at least a year of work. The experiment was of remarkable value therefore for the fact that Baucher accomplished it after only 13 days of exercise, with horses as disparate as those of the *lancers and cuirassiers*.

Little by little an increasing number of officers from the Brigade and the *Garde Municipale* came to take lessons and declare themselves convinced of the superiority of the new procedures over those of the Ordinance. A very few amongst the old zealots for written orders and formalism dared to have reservations about the disorder brought about by instruction with procedures so little favorable to discipline, and they observed that, after all, the horses that had been submitted to the experiment were far from being fresh, and that their previous training had been advanced enough that one could think it not useful to send them to the Depot. But these critiques formulated with moderation, were lost in the wave of enthusiasm that was aroused in all the young officers who were seduced by the brilliant success of the experiment, and more yet by the rapid efficacy of the expeditious procedures that allowed one to achieve success in so little time.

Precise and detailed, the report from the Commission, written up by Commandant de Novital, naturally recommended the adoption of the new method, insisting on the advantages of the so important reduction in the time that had been necessary to confirm the training up until then, and of the alleviation that the method brought to one of the heaviest constraints on the Cavalry.

Experiment in the New Method at the Paris Garrison

*(Lithograph from "Guide de l'ami du cheval"
(Guide of the friend of the horse) by Lancosme-Brèves)*

Baucher on his part addressed a letter to General Oudinot drawing his attention to the imperious necessity that his method be able to be introduced into the Army to educate instructors capable of teaching in the troop.[46]

---

46   He added to this letter some criticisms of the horses' tack and the riders' equipment. The principal ones were addressed to the attachment point for the stirrup bar, fixed too forward on the saddle, nearly directly under the pommel. The rider's feet were therefore constantly drawn forward from their regular position and the legs could not have contact with the horse's flanks except by kicks,

As for General Oudinot, he addressed his report forthwith to the Minister, and pressed to strike while the iron was still hot, requesting in the first place, the immediate organization at Baucher's *manège* of a course for student instructor officers designated by twos from each Regiment of Cavalry stationed in a radius of 25 leagues[47] around Paris, and in the second place, of an experiment on a greater scale to be carried out with the 4 regiments of dragoons stationed at Camp Lunéville.

He wrote his report in terms most laudatory of the new method's author, and of the results that he had obtained. Carried away by the ardor of his conviction, the General went perhaps even a little beyond strict reality, affirming that this method had been applied to "completely ignorant young horses."

Surely the General had probably been charged by his colleagues on the Cavalry Committee to express their unanimous opinion. Nevertheless, one can only be surprised at the weak part played by this highly learned assembly in an experiment that arose directly from its mandate, and to encounter, in no part of the correspondence exchanged on the subject of this experiment, the name of General de Sparre, Vice-President[48] of the Committee, and more senior by *twenty years* than General Oudinot in the rank of Lieutenant-General[49]....

The course for Captain and Lieutenant student-instructors decided on by the Minister began on the 1st of June under the

---

aggravated by the excessive use of the spur of which the shaft was no less than 7 centimeters.

The height of the kit carried on the front of the saddle was such that the rider had to maintain his hand above the position in which he should keep it.

It is to be remarked that the necessary rectifications were eventually applied to these defects, but it required no less than 30 years for the War Office to get around to it.

47 Translator's note: league: the distance a person or a horse can walk in an hour.

48 The President of the Cavalry Committee was the Duc d'Orléans, Commander-in-Chief of the Army.

49 General de Sparre had been promoted to Lieutenant-General in 1814, General Oudinot had been promoted to the same rank in 1835.

command of a Chef d'Escadrons whose report was not any less favorable to the new method than that of General Oudinot.

We read there notably: "The oral explanations were nearly always given to each rider in private and then the application on the horse was immediately demanded. M. Baucher only left the officer to whom he was speaking after being assured by questions that his explanation was understood. He solicited the observations of each rider and gave to each principle that he had put forward all of the development requested. *This manner of giving a lesson appeared strange in the beginning; it was new for us who up until then had received and given lessons in equitation in the manège by explanations given in a loud voice and from which explanations each student had to profit according to his intelligence. So, not only were the equitation principles new, but the manner of teaching was also new.*"

"The officers had not all arrived with the belief that anyone had something to teach them. After around 25 lessons, all of them without exception had understood the method and recognized the superiority of M. Baucher's principles."

"I believe that we should bring up to at least 2 months the time consecrated to lessons."

And this last observation, even so modest, leads to observing that not General Oudinot, nor Commandant de Novital, nor Baucher himself, appeared to conceive of the least doubt about the permanence of the results achieved in thirteen days of training for the troop horses, and in 39 for the instruction of the officers who had to train their own horses at the same time.

At Camp Lunéville, two brigades of cavalry had been brought together and for their instruction had been placed under the direction of General Oudinot, who resolved to regulate the experiment prescribed in such a way that the presentation of his results would be transformed into a dazzling public demonstration, destined to convince opinion and the press of the overwhelming superiority of the new method over the old errors.[50]

---

50   Grandstands for 6,000 people were constructed on the esplanade where the presentation was to be held in front of the chateau.

The General excelled in the organization of these spectacular demonstrations, and he had acquired great experience at it in Saumur during the six years of his command. In 1828, he conceived and organized, at the occasion of the visit of the Duchesse de Berry, the first carrousel at the School, the success of which rang throughout Europe. The exercises that he made up were considered at the time, by all knowledgeable people, as an acme barely imaginable in the instruction of an *élite* troop, and the execution of these exercises as a tour de force, realizable only with chosen officers trained as unequaled specialists, mounted on horses whose dressage exceeded by far anything that was possible in the regiments.

The General intended to show that the new method allowed getting to the same results in a few weeks, not only with officers, but with riders of the ranks on troop horses. His program consisted of three distinct carrousels, one for officers, another for *sous-officiers*, and the third executed by two squadrons constituted: one mounted on older horses chosen from among the best trained in the old manner, the other on only young horses trained in a few weeks according to the new method.

The preparation began on the 1st of June under the direction of Baucher's son, Baucher himself having been retained in Paris for the student instructor course. The Duc d'Orléans, Commanding General of the Army, announced his inspection for 20 July. From the beginning of the month of July, with the training being considered complete, the rehearsals of the various carrousels had begun, and everything allowed the General to count on success when there was a catastrophe that plunged the Royal Family, France, and the Army into consternation: on 13 July, the Duc d'Orléans was killed by jumping from his carriage when his horses got carried away, and all of Baucher's hopes were taken away with his fall. Of course all military celebrations were cancelled. Two months later the Duc de Nemours, in the course of an inspection of the East, during a visit to Camp Lunéville, was presented the squadron of young horses prepared for the carrousel and he deigned to make known his satisfaction with the results obtained.

He was accompanied by General de Sparre. General Oudinot who had been *attaché* to the Duc d'Orléans had probably been held up in Paris by the official mourning and his presence is not reported during the Duc de Nemours' visit.

Now it so happened that General de Sparre had come to make the annual inspection of the Cavalry School, where Commandant de Novital had on his part proceeded to a second experiment in Baucher's method, and the General doubtlessly had not failed to make the Prince aware of the impressions that he had brought back.

As soon as he had returned to Saumur, Commandant de Novital hurried to organize the trials that he had been charged with as a result of the one in Paris. He put together a preliminary lesson with the *Sous-Maîtres* riding *manège* horses recently assigned to the remount for the instruction squadron. The *Écuyer en Chef* displayed his usual exuberant and precipitated activity in this organization, and the gaps in his impetuous character did not fail to provoke, once again, the difficulties that came up too frequently in his direction of the *manège* and military exercises. He saw with discontent most of his *sous-officiers* distracted from their service, turned upside down without any consideration by the *Écuyer en Chef* himself, and the *sous-officiers* themselves dreaded their superior officer's well known severity and verbal violence.

Commandant de Novital probably had acquired a sufficient knowledge of the procedures of the new method, however much shortened, but his excessive temperament separated him dangerously from the advised prudence that Baucher had proven to have in the experiments in Paris. Far from the spirit of moderation that the Master had largely brought to the teaching of his theories, the Commandant envisioned their application with the entire rigor of a technique to which he was known to bring temperamental storms.

A characteristic detail permits some judgment: While Baucher in his letter to General Oudinot recommended the shortening of the shafts of the riders' spurs, the memo from Commandant de Novital on the organization of the experiment finished with this sentence: "The *sous-officiers* must be given spurs with pointed rowels."

The results obtained from the first run were excellent. All the difficult horses that formed it were brought to complete submission, save two that were in reality infirm.[51]

In the second course, Commandant de Novital had many disappointments. Many of the horses persisted in "disputing" the spurs, whether by holding back or by kicking at the boot. On the whole the results produced very little satisfaction.

There was nothing surprising in the difference in the two results. The corps of *Sous-Maîtres* was at that time a remarkable lineup. All of them subsequently made a name for themselves in their equestrian careers. One of them, Guérin, was one of the best *Écuyers en Chef* at the Cavalry School fifteen years later. Another, Dijon, fulfilled the same function at Saint-Cyr and at the *École d'État-Major*. A third, Ducas, became Master of the *Manège* at Bordeaux, was one of the inventors of work on the whip, etc.... etc.... And by then the *Sous-Maîtres* had been accustomed for a long time to the command of their *Écuyer en Chef* who liked to direct their work and their instruction himself. His furies, which they knew would be gone the next day without a grudge, no longer troubled them.

As for the s*ous-officiers* from the Cadre, they were not in the least familiar with dressage and did not ride except for service. Even their good will, over the course of the experiment, did not exceed their equestrian skill, which was thin. As it happened often for the other ranks, the conflict that had reigned for more than twenty years between their service and that of the *manège* took on the form of sullen opposition. Their officers' malcontent with the transgressions by the *Écuyer en Chef* was not unknown to them. They were also indifferent to the success of the new system.

---

51 The one who fell down at any moment, very frequently when being mounted, eventually suffered from vertigo and killed himself in a crisis in the infirmary. The other who lay down at the least contact of the legs was recognized later as suffering from "immobility" and had to be put down.

Even in the *manège*, there was far from unanimity on the value of the method so ardently advocated by the *Écuyer en Chef* who, following his habits, held opinions entirely apart from the experience of his two civilian *écuyers*, Commandant Rousselet[52] and Monsieur de Saint-Ange. For having only assisted at the dressage lessons from afar, these two enlightened practitioners had none the less observed the violence of the fierce battles from which the horses left with bloody flanks, probably conquered, but like a wild cat in front of the hot iron of the tamer. Commandant Rousselet finished by coming out from behind his reserve and, in his indignation, he had just been about to pronounce the word "butchery" when his colleague, Saint-Ange, spoke of "ferocity." These expressions, surely excessive, naturally made a tour of the School and found a complying echo among certain elements of the Cadre.

On the other hand, the student officers who followed the School's various courses were taken by an irresistible fancy for the Baucher method. Each one carried under his arm a freshly cut example of the new gospel and a new pair of spurs on their heels. Passage, piaffe, and pirouettes formed the exclusive and passionate subject of conversations. They were "grinding away" in all the discrete corners of the School and its environs or even barricaded in the stable. Horses that had shown themselves docile and peaceable suddenly developed obstinate rebelliousness and the riders' kicking flooded the Squadron School (with blood).

Assailed by protestations from the Military Instruction Service, General de Prévot, who was in command of the School, was very perplexed. His predecessor, General Oudinot, had retained a right of scrutiny of the school that extended quite far because of his personal situation close to the Prince, Commander-in-Chief of the Army. Since everyone was announcing the approaching adoption of the new method, for which General Oudinot had been the protagonist, it was very difficult for his successor to take measures that could be interpreted as unfavor-

---

52 Commandant Rousselet had been *Chef d'Escadrons* under the Empire and they kept the title for him, well that he had been retired for 25 years and was a civilian *écuyer*.

able to its propagation, and to modify arrangements on which he moreover had hardly been consulted.

In order to attend to the most urgent thing first, he brought back the interdiction, which had fallen into disuse, for all the school's students against riding alone except on personal authorization accorded by the Director of Military Exercises, who from there on systematically refused, and the students did not fail to pretend themselves victims of the "anti-Baucherists cabal."

Happily, the annual inspection at the end of the course saved General Prévot from embarrassment. It took place a few days after the Duc d'Orléans' accident, and was carried out by General de Sparre, who took heed of the reports from the Commandant of the School on the experiments made and on their results.

THE FINAL EXPERIMENT AT SAUMUR

In General Oudinot's projects, the trials by Commandant de Novital constituted but a sort of prelude to the final experiment that needed to be finished before the end of the school year.

The death of the Duc d'Orléans and the delay that the resulting delay had brought to the trials at Lunéville, and then the interminable floods of the Loire at the end of the winter, delayed until the month of February 1843 the course that, according to ministerial orders, Baucher was supposed to teach at the Cavalry School.

At the school, the conditions for the new test were not at all unfavorable. The return to their service of the *Sous-Officiers* and the horses for Military Instruction had calmed down the more ardent adversaries of the Method, many of whom moreover had left Saumur in the normal course of advancement. Two promotions (classes) of officers had been replaced in the course of instruction and the state of morale at the School was at the beginning of its annual renewal. At the *Manège*, the civilian *Écuyers* remained hostile to the new system, and the military *Écuyers*, Captains and Lieutenants, were divided into two tendencies, while the *Écuyer en Chef* and the *Sous-Maîtres* persisted in their enthusiasm for the Baucher method, justified, one might say, by the remarkable results that they had obtained. They were more than ever pressed into the stands for the parades by the Cadre, where the *Écuyer en Chef*, by the perfection of the dressage of his horse, Ourphaly, and the brilliance of his presentation eclipsed all of his subordinates.

But in Paris, the situation was singularly changed, and even if one could imagine the origin of its development to be from strongly motivated suspicions, it is difficult to justify them entirely from irrefutable documents.

No criticism, unfavorable to the method, of the experiments in Paris and Lunéville had been made in any official or unofficial publication. On the contrary, the *"Spectateur Militaire,"* of which the attachments to the Minister were not dubious, published many very laudatory articles on the results obtained by Baucher.

However, the arrangements made by General de Sparre, who was charged with the "inspection" of the course at Saumur, for the preparation and execution of this test, along with his attitude in regard to Baucher, were witness to a surprising hostility and an inexplicable lack of consideration.

These arrangements and this attitude are only known to us, to tell the truth, by the exposé that Baucher himself published in a chapter added to his work under the title "The Truth about my Mission to Saumur," and one could doubt the exactitude of this exposé if the least challenge had been raised to it. But there was nothing. From 1842 to 1845, this chapter appeared in 6 successive editions of the method, yet no rectification of its contents, no challenge, not on the heart of the matter nor on the form, has ever been published.

One must admit therefore the reality of the facts exposed by Baucher, and their singularity is such that it appears necessary to bring them up in their chronological order.

Before quitting Paris for Saumur, Baucher presented himself to General de Sparre to ask him for his instructions. The General gave him none and announced that he would join Baucher very shortly at Saumur.

On arriving at Saumur, Baucher received from General de Prévot the communication of a "manual," addressed to the Commandant of the School by General de Sparre, as an "instruction to serve for the organization and conduct of the course by M. Baucher." This manual contained only a few truncated and distorted extracts from the progression followed in the preceding experiments on the training of young horses. Baucher observed that this manual, of which the wording was totally strange, could not be used as a base for a course designed to make the whole of his method understood by officers assigned to teach it afterwards. He refused to give his course in such conditions and announced his departure, but General de Prévot asked him to put it off until General de Sparre's arrival.

Baucher waited for this arrival for four days. Over the course of a two-hour interview, General de Sparre addressed to Baucher, whatever could have been the context, many stupefying sentences, of which the General never contested the terms:

"We want your method, but we don't want equitation...

"Do one thing, and we will be in accord, do not speak of legs in your courses..."

Finally General de Sparre "lifted his interdiction and gave General de Prévot the order to 'let M. Baucher do as he intended.'" The course began on 16 February, and was to last three months. There were a considerable number of students. The course consisted of 24 officers from School Headquarters and 48 Captains and Lieutenants detached from the corps of troops. Baucher, aided by his son, had to form five groups, for whom the daily lessons lasted of one and a half hours.

Furthermore, in order to be able to work some difficult horses alone, and to give the personal counseling that they demanded, Baucher had to spend 9 hours in the *manège* every day, in a glacial cold.

General de Sparre, during the first 2 days, attended several lessons, about two hours each day, and then left for Paris. The Commission, presided over by General de Prévot, met each week to establish the minutes of the obtained results, and it's much studied and strongly motivated appreciation was clearly favorable to the adoption of the new system.

On 25 March, General de Sparre addressed to the Commandant of the School a note de service fixing the end of the course for 1 April, which reduced its duration by half. He came back to Saumur to make a last "inspection" of about 2 hours, over the course of which he contented himself with "paging through the register of the deliberations of the Commission, without questioning any of the student officers, who, except for 5 out of 72, had in their report to the Commission manifested entire satisfaction with the teaching they had received and the results obtained.

Finally, General de Sparre addressed to Baucher a letter not less surprising than his attitude in the whole run of this affair. He began by transmitting to Baucher, as well as to his son, the testimony of the satisfaction that the Minister had *prescribed* him to address to them. Then, coming back to his distinction between training (dressage) and equitation, he "regretted not having been informed about the development given by Baucher to his teaching," avowed himself insufficiently instructed in the method to judge its more or less efficacy, and finally recognized that "the results obtained and the training of young horses had been in general satisfactory."

To crown these incoherences, General de Sparre issued an "Order of the Day" to be posted at the School, forbidding the practice of the method "with the exception of the principles concerning young horses."

The conduct of General de Sparre[53] would be incomprehensible if the difficulties of the situation in which he found himself did not allow one to find an explanation. In all likelihood, the General did not have any firm opinion of equestrian matters. He received his instruction in horsemanship on the roads of Europe,

---

53 Grandson of one of the best of Charles XII's generals, General de Sparre had begun his military career in the King of Sweden's Foot Guards. He had served in the French Army in all the campaigns of the Empire. Did perhaps his knowledge of our language present some lacking?

between two victories, and like his colleague on the Committee, General Desmichels, probably thought that "the equitation of Austerlitz still suffices." But Marshal Soult, Minister of War, was of a radically opposed opinion. In one of his Instructions for the Cavalry, he had written a sentence that has remained celebrated in the history of this arm, "Certainly, equitation is not everything in the Cavalry, but all is nothing without it."

There is no doubt that the famous guide-manual sent to Saumur by General de Sparre that he so easily retired in the face the Baucher's protests, had not received approbation from the Minister, no more than had the distinction between training and equitation, on which the General did not insist anymore.

But the Duc de Nemours, having become a member of the Cavalry Committee upon the death of his brother, had rapidly made prevalent the equestrian ideas of his Master, the Vicomte d'Aure, and the Vicomte, having written in his *"Observations sur la Méthode Baucher"* (*Observations on the Baucher Method*), "I am not at all a trainer of horses," had created this famous distinction between training and equitation that General de Sparre had tried to oppose to Baucher's teaching projects.

Caught between the princely hammer and the ministerial anvil, General de Sparre was forced to satisfy the Duke without entering into open opposition with the Minister, whose firmness was well known.

It was a thankless task and it was no doubt without gaiety of heart that the General had accepted the sacrificial role that he had to play and that the opposition press did not fail to severely criticize.

Two brochures avenged Baucher's disappointments. One, by Clément Thomas, harshly attacked, in the tone of a merciless prosecutional summing up, the General, the Duke and the regime. The other, in an ironic style, lined up those with a sense of humor on Baucher's side. It had for author, the Baron de Cornieu, and for title, *"What if Baucher Had Never Existed."*

Baucherism, according to the facetious Baron, was not but a distortion of Christianity, destroyer of the old religions. Baucher was nothing other than a mythic figure substituted for that of

Jesus. His well-known faithful were the twelve apostles. After the voyage in Italy, a memory confused with the flight into Egypt, the coming of Baucher to Paris figured for the entry into Jerusalem, etc., etc. Finally, the experience at Saumur was not but the temptation of Jesus by Satan. Dragging Baucher up to the highest dormer of the hayloft, where they had beneath their eyes the panorama of the School, the same as the Devil had transported Jesus to the summit of the mountain, de Sparre-Satan said to Baucher, "Speak not of legs, and all this shall be yours...!"

Baucher returned to Paris sickened. His dearest hope, the adoption of his method by the Army that he had made the goal of his life, was more than compromised. To the devotion and unselfishness that he had given so brilliant proof, they had responded with discourteous procedures and vexing measures. He was profoundly wounded and remained so all his life. Disdaining recriminations, he remained estranged from the protests by his partisans, and contented himself with inserting into his new edition of his work the exposé of the events at Saumur mentioned above, of which no one ever contested the exactitude. Yet he deleted this chapter after the death of General de Sparre, conserving to the end an attitude full of dignity that he never abandoned.

Outside of General de Sparre, whose conduct could be found to be in attenuated circumstances for want of excuses, it is to the Duc de Nemours that we must attribute the responsibility for the maneuvering and lack of consideration to which Baucher fell victim. The least that one could say of these procedures is that they were regrettable, but must we equally regret the irreducible opposition by the Prince to the introduction of Baucher's method into the Army? It certainly seems that we should not. The consequences of putting the new method into practice in the Army would have been very probably disastrous, because it was uniquely under the immediate and continuous direction of Baucher or his son that the experiments gave good results, the persistence of which, besides, had not been able to be verified for lack of time. Even conducted by a teaching professional as skillful as Commandant de Novital, the first tests at Saumur were very far from having obtained much success. What would have happened with lessons given in the regiments by instructors themselves with so little training? In the ardor of their faith, these neophytes would not have failed to apply, with a fanatical stubbornness, the dangerous rigors of the method as of 1842, infinitely too delicate for the equestrian aptitude of the average military rider.

For some successes there were doubtlessly recorded a great number of grave failures, provoking a reaction not less violent than the passion for the new system. The incertitude and the disarray would weaken anew the already precarious instruction in the cavalry.

Whatever were the faults of the Duc de Nemours in his consideration of Baucher, it is very probable that he, without knowing too much why, had reason, regarding the Army, for his opposition to the adoption of the new method. One could go farther and think that in the end, Baucher's method benefited from these measures that were doubtlessly wounding to its author, but that conferred on him the warrant of political victim, always strongly appreciated in France. Marshal Soult did not give in to the wishes of the Duc de Nemours without a long resistance, and it was only in 1845 that the interdiction ordered in 1843 by General de Sparre for the School at Saumur was extended by the Marshal to the Corps of Troops and then under the very form that permitted widely enlarged interpretations.

The Prince still had to wait for the retirement of the Marshal in 1847 to get from his successor the assignment of the Vicomte d'Aure to Saumur as *Écuyer en Chef*. During these four years, time brought its pacifying influence to the ardor of those enthusiastic for the method, and like those for the opposition, hardly reflective. A selection operated among the officers who had been instructed so hurriedly by Baucher. The maladroit and the opportunists abandoned the method at the first lack of success. The continuers and the more gifted persisted in the new way, applying all their skill to avoid failures. It was their sensible prudence that preceded the gradual preparation for a "subdued Baucherism" that later allowed its fusion with part of the Vicomte d'Aure's procedures, and it was their wisdom that later led Baucher himself on the way to his "Second Manner."

CHAPTER VIII -
IN THE CAPITALS OF EUROPE

Disappointed in his dearest hopes, wounded in his justified self-esteem, Baucher resolved to pursue the success that had been stolen from him, and by a detour, to command the achievement that had escaped him.

By carrying the fight for the propagation of his equestrian principles out of France, he counted, by provoking at first the admiration of crowds, on obtaining the conversion afterward of the appropriate people to his method, from which the adoption by foreign armies would not fail to bring France to revise a judgment that he could not believe to be without appeal.

The German States had kept the cult of equestrian art, and the reputation of the Prussian Cavalry remained unequaled in the armies over the Rhine. But now Dejean, who with Franconi was a former director of the Cirque des Champs-Élysées, was on the way to recruiting a large troupe for a long tour of Germany, where he had already often led the Circus that bore his name, which was well known in all the capitals. He hastened to grant to Baucher an agreement advantageous to each of them, and said Rul, "the unrecognized innovator left his ungracious homeland with the hope to return in triumph."

In Berlin, his success was at first dazzling; he had taken along the *élite* of his horses. Partisan, Captaine, and Buridan were at the highest point of their careers. Their work was of a perfection and variety that defied any comparison with the German circus professionals. The Berlin public was more aware of the subtleties of equestrian art than that of Paris, and even if the execution of that art in the new manner sometimes came up against the principles taken to be sacrosanct in the German *manèges*, the virtuosity of the artist, who mastered the difficulties of execution better than any of his predecessors had approached, nevertheless aroused the enthusiasm of the amazed spectators.

In witness to his "great satisfaction," King Frederick-William presented Baucher with a snuffbox "of admirable work." No less flattering distinctions were accorded to him by the Courts of Saxony and Hannover. In the Southern States, as in Austria where equitation was more directly subject to the influence of the Spanish Riding School, his presentations were more questioned, and his method aroused passionate controversy, but the immense majority of the public remained favorable.

Everywhere influential figures, military and civilian, were enthusiastic about the new principles and followed the course of Baucher's tour. Here and there a few enterprising officers, without waiting for orders that seemed that they must be given any day, hurried to pass the benefit of their new knowledge to the troops placed under their direct command.

During this time, Rul, the well loved disciple, untiring propagandist of the new equestrian religion, evangelized the infidels over the Rhine in the cities that were not part of the itinerary of the Cirque Dejean, or where, after the departure of the troupe, he came in to complete the barely sketched out instruction for the newly converted. But this was a much compromised missionary! Reveler, card gambler, always ready to fight, he got himself expelled from Dresden after having wounded two adversaries in dueling in the same week. In Vienna, he incurred the angry condemnation of the clergy by organizing spirit séances, for which he had a passion, and so the propagation of the Baucherist faith suffered...

In brief, around 1850, after six annual tours of the Circus, several squadrons, even some regiments, had received the new training in various States with more or less success, but no official adoption of the method had taken place in any army.

Before the fall of the July Monarchy, the German governments, even the most disposed to the new method, had not failed to seek information about the reasons why it was rejected by the

French army. The declared opposition by the Duc de Nemours, brother-in-law to the Princes of Wurtenburg and Saxony by the marriage of his sisters, himself the spouse of a German Princess, had struck a severe blow against the opinion of the Courts and Headquarters that had been at first favorable to the adoption of the new system. After the days of February 1848 and their violent repercussions in all of Germany, Baucherism coming from Paris took on a demagogic odor at the moment when there arose the inevitable reaction. "It's the equitation of the *sans-culottes*," said Count Grünn, first adjutant to the Emperor, and, so baptized, the new method everywhere lost its last chance for official adoption.

Baucher was profoundly affected. The goal to which he had directed his whole life turned out to be permanently inaccessible. His character was embittered again and even his activities suffered for a time. Caught in the chains of his contractual obligations, he continued to tour Europe, sometimes with the Cirque Dejean, sometimes with the Cirque Soullier. From then on, shrunken to the dimensions of the *piste*, his equestrian ideal moved more and more away from the realities of practical equitation, and little by little, it came to slide from the practice of art into that of "craft." Hurried and very nearly slap-dash training let him renew his performances according to the terms of his contract, but it was to the detriment of their artistic value.

Neglecting the fundamental airs of true *Haute École*, he began to make predominant in his "numbers" the "*gambades*" suitable for delighting the mass of philistines, the "fanciful gaits," as he called them, based on "*jambettes*" and semblances of *rassembler*, the "Spanish" walk and trot, the canters on three legs (forward and back), the *lançades*, all that his adversaries scornfully called, not without reason, "*haute école* on the cheap."

His returns to France were hard. He shortened his stays in Paris and took refuge in the provinces, where some of his students succeeded in taking his lessons if he believed those students to have found the sacred fire. With that, his teaching regained all of its persuasive and captivating force, and their progress impassioned him just as at the heroic time of his career.

So it was that a young lieutenant from the Guides, at Lyon, came to inspire in Baucher an interest and soon affection to which only the death of the Master would put an end.

He was the future General l'Hotte.

THE ACCIDENT

In 1855, in the course of a stay in Paris, Baucher was the victim of an accident that should have cost him his life. While he was working a horse on the *piste* at the Cirque des Champs-Élysées, the chandelier detached from the arch and fell on him.

When they picked him up, his right leg was broken, his hip and knee dislocated with grave contusions on the upper part of his torso, his shoulders, and his lower back. Only his head came out without a scratch from the entanglement of gas conduits, branches, and candelabra of the enormous apparatus.

Having remained imperturbably calm over the course of his rescue, which he directed himself, Baucher was immobilized for long months, and his equestrian career appeared very compromised. One could have believed that this new blow would have led to the bitterness of despair.

There was nothing of the sort. Despite his suffering and the uncertainty of his being able to ride again, this painful accident had a very happy influence on his morale and on the evolution of his talent.

The news of his accident rapidly made a tour around Paris. In relating it, the press found its enthusiastic accents of former days again recalling the celebrity of this wounded man. Baucher's friends came in crowds in witness to their sympathy, and many of his adversaries made a point of testifying to their esteem by coming to hear his news. The artist's pathological sensitivity found in this attentiveness the satisfaction that he had been deprived of for a long time. He was greatly comforted.

And then his military students brought him very encouraging news. At Saumur, Commandant Guérin had succeeded Comte d'Aure. He was the former *Sous-Maître* who, thirteen years earlier, had been so very successful at the School in the trial of the new method, for which he had not hidden his preference. Without contesting the value of d'Aure's method, which he had studied in depth for seven years under the very direction of its author, Commandant Guérin prudently modified the teaching of the School, making the essential practices of the Baucher method a greater and greater part of it.

Moreover, the interdiction that had officially struck against the Baucher method was put to bed. In much of the Corps of Troops, those adept at Baucherism practiced it openly after having adapted it with time to military goals and means. In the Paris Garrison very particularly, the success of certain training practices in the regiments drew attention from the Command to the officers that had directed those practices and who were found to be students of Baucher.

In their conversations with the Master, whom they came to see in his little apartment on the Rue Amelot, these officers described the difficulties that they had run into, their attempts to surmount them or to get around them, their disappointments and their successes. From these observations, made in a line of practice that he could have only anticipated thirteen years beforehand, Baucher regained contact with the realities of the daily use of the horse. His inventive spirit fortunately parted from the artificial conditions of spectacular equitation to finally come back to fix itself on the necessity for a simplification that would make the method accessible to all, to rule out its dangers without harming its efficacy. It was therefore in the plaster that immobilized him that Baucher began to conceive his "Second Manner."

When, after a long convalescence, he could think about getting back onto a horse, his physical capabilities were greatly reduced. The exceptional power of his legs was gravely weakened, and the continuity of their pressure rapidly became insupportable. These difficulties fortunately brought him closer to common riders. They allowed him to experiment with new aids, suggested by his ingenuity, in conditions for applying them that would be much closer to those in which were found the new students that would go on to benefit from them.

CHAPTER IX - THE SECOND MANNER

It is common usage in the equestrian literature to give the name "Second Manner" to the arrangement of the procedures as recommended by Baucher in the 12th edition of his Method, appearing in 1864.

In reality, this "manner" is only the last of the perfections that the Master had continuously brought to his work over the course of his long career.

Certainly one does not find any trace of the Second Manner in the 11 earlier editions because they were nearly a copy of the 1842 text in conformance with clauses in Baucher's contract with his editors, which did not expire until 1863. However, it suffices to go through the works of his students to find, in their chronological order, the modifications that the Master brought to the system in his oral teaching, reproduced in the works of Daudel (1857), Gerhardt (1859), and Wachter (1862), for example.

On this characteristic of continued creation, which threw off certain of his students in whom the flexibility of mind and the resources of talent were not sufficient to permit them to get past a certain stage in which they found themselves stopped, General l'Hotte wrote:

> "Baucher scoured the art to its ultimate secrets, rolled back the limits, and delivered himself to incessant research, bringing out an uninterrupted succession of discoveries that made him an innovator of a fecundity without example."

One can only subscribe to this judgment without reserve, but we must bring up that the search for the best and the pursuit of the ideal were not alone in determining this progressive evolution. In part, the concern to make the application of the method easier for riders of modest aptitude and ambition, and on the other hand, the impossibility, in which Baucher found himself after his accident, of employing his aids with the same power as before certainly contributed to the modification of the means that he had used up until then.

For it was certainly only to a modification of the means that he applied himself. All the essentials of the method, its principles, its spirit, remain intact in the "Second Manner."

The essentials of the system are the *"mise en main"* and the *"effet d'ensemble"* that remained at its base in 1864 just as in 1842, but the means to obtain each are modified in their nature, their combination, and the measure of their application.

For the *mise en main*, the lightening of the forehand, previously sought only by the *ramener*, is now sought by a preliminary lifting of the neck that, just as for the *ramener*, provokes a shifting of weight from front to back. With the neck raised, as soon as the jaw loosens, a similar degree of lightness is obtained almost without any *ramener*, at least with a *ramener* much less accentuated than if it had to determine by itself the shortening of the lever arm of the neck and the lightening of the forehand that would result.

Now the lifting of the neck is obtained much more easily and rapidly than is the *ramener*. By this new procedure, the rider is therefore able to obtain from his horse, with much less dexterity and time than the First Manner requires, a position of the whole body that assures him an equilibrium that is quite sufficient for the needs of practical equitation.

The *ramener* however remains indispensable as soon as the rider wants to increase his domination, whether to master a difficult horse or to start artistic equitation. To obtain the *ramener* from then on, Baucher gave up brining back the horse's nose progressively towards his chest, as he had in his preliminary flexions. On the contrary, in the new manner, it is the progressive advance of the horse's body toward his head, fixed in place by the rider who little by little provokes, as general suppleness grows, the bending of the neck and the verticality of the head. So obtained, the *ramener* ceases to be independent of the position of the whole body of the horse. It is linked on the contrary to the beginning of a *rassembler* that is always ready to exert itself in the direction of the horse's initial movement that has produced it: *forward*.

As for the *effet d'ensemble*, the means to obtain it are modified only by a refinement of precautions in accustoming the horse to the pressure of the legs and then to the spur, and by the eventual use of the cavesson to curb defenses during that progression.

But the *effet d'ensemble*, which, in the First Manner, constitutes the *normal and habitual* means to re-establish lost lightness, is not used anymore with this goal in mind, except when the resistance becomes one of "morale," as one could say, and turns into a defense. Consequently, even in this case, the *effet d'ensemble* remains within the limits to which from then onward it was assigned: that of the *ultimate* means of domination.

In the new manner, it is the hand alone that is charged with re-establishing lightness, and Baucher distinguished two ways of using it to this end; the half-halt, to remedy the surcharge of weight on the forehand, and the vibration, to make the muscular contractions "melt."

The essential of the new manner is precisely this systematic rejection of the continuous simultaneous use of the hand and the legs, from where comes the formula:

"Hand without legs, legs without hand."

Now, the accord of the aids when they are used simultaneously constitutes the greatest difficulty in equitation. Order compromised by an excess of the hand, for example, could apparently be re-established by an action of the legs, but only apparently. In the most favorable case, the rider will nonetheless have provoked an untimely *rassembler* that in no way corresponds to his initial intention and, without his having wanted it, this faulty *rassembler* modifies the balance of his mount and becomes a new source of difficulties by its eventual disaccord with the work demanded of the horse.

Also this combination of the aids leads too often, according to Baucher's expression, "to making one of the faults pay for the other," to the detriment of balance and order. In removing this "contest," by prescribing to the contrary the application of the formula "legs without hand, hand without legs," the Second Manner did away with, in one fell swoop, the all too frequent occasions of their disaccord.

With the hand alone assuming the regulation and distribution of the action, the legs have the sole charge of producing impulsion, and to make sure that this is quite so, *even in the effet d'ensemble*, once the submission is obtained, as soon as the hand lowers its barrier, it must end with a frank depart determined by maintaining the pressure of the legs, increased if needed, and even confirmed by an attack of the spurs in case of hesitation or laziness.

It is there that is found a perfection of the greatest importance that leads to the disappearance of the stumbling block on which have come to grief so many students of the First Manner: this disposition of the horse "to go to sleep on the spur" after the *effet d'ensemble*, pointed out by General l'Hotte in his "portrait of a Baucherised horse in 1849."

For the "utilitarian" rider, the application of the new formula therefore consists of a simplification and a guarantee, the scope of which is considerable. For the *écuyer*, the advantages of the Second Manner are yet much more important. In all dressage work that does not include the *rassembler* and in which the precision of the movement constitutes the essential form of the art, the isolated use of an aid puts in clear light any fault that the rider might commit, whereas in the "contest" of many aids, this fault would be "drowned" in the confusion of actions and their effects.

When this same aid is used alone, and is solely responsible for an eventual disorder, it is therefore by a correction brought only to the aid's own action that the disorder can be remedied right away and be avoided afterward according to the experience and progress of the rider's skill. To ride, for example, a perfectly round, exactly placed and sized volte on the indications of a single rein, it is necessary to have in the actions of the hand used by itself, correctness, finesse, and dexterity that the simultaneous use of two reins and two legs does not permit one to discover and even less to acquire with the system of compensations and compromises that such use includes.

When, as it goes on, seeking the *rassembler* necessitates the simultaneous use of the legs and the hand, the refinement of their actions that was previously acquired over the course of their isolated use puts at the disposition of the *écuyer* a range of nuances in their effects that permits him not only to avoid any disaccord, but to obtain the harmony of a perfect accord.

Roughed out in the 12th edition of his method in 1864, the new manner was clearly laid out in the 13th in 1867. It was later explained with all the development it had attained by 1870, for all branches of equitation, in the "Last Teachings of Baucher" published by General Faverot de Kerbrech (see Faverot de Kerbrech, *Methodical Dressage of the Riding Horse...*, Xenophon Press 2010). In reading this admirable work, as clear as it is precise, but that did not appear until 1891, it is not prohibited to think that, despite the certain fidelity of the student to the teaching of his Master, the General's own personal experience after 20 years of practice in the new manner had not failed to contribute to the perfection of this brilliant exposé of the last thoughts of Baucher.

General de Kerbrech also described a reduced and simplified progression of the new procedures that is sufficient for the preparation of a horse for the outdoors in a brochure that appeared in 1907 under the title *"Dressage du cheval de dehors"* (*Dressage of the Outdoor Horse*, see *Methodical Dressage of the Riding Horse and Dressage of the Outdoor Horse*, Xenophon Press 2010). Before him, Lenoble du Teil had treated the same subject, but with 1less detail.

Finally, it is necessary to point out that Rul, in 1870, published a small volume entitled *"Progression méthodique du dressage à l'aide d'un simple filet de tous les chevaux de la Cavalerie"* (*Methodical Progression of Dressage with the Aid of a Simple Bridoon for all Cavalry Horses*). It was a very succinct exposé of the new method. It is above all worthy of interest because of the fact that it was purchased from its author by the Minister of War, despite the interdiction against the Baucher Method, which has never been lifted.

CHAPTER X - THE LAST YEARS

Baucher continued to teach up until 1870. The management of the Cirque gave him a small pension, continued to feed his horses, and left the *piste* at his disposal for part of the morning. In the afternoon, he gave lessons at different *manèges* around Paris where he also boarded some horses. He hardly gave any group lessons except for a few officers, notably those from the *École d'État-Major*, or *élite* troops like those of the *Cent Gardes*, whose instruction had been confided to him by the Emperor upon the formation of their squadron. His greatest preference was for lessons particularly reserved to a few students of choice, those most gifted, the only ones that he initiated into the difficulties of *Haute École*.

He still rode, but tired quickly in the saddle and could no longer dream of performing in public without it costing him, however little. For the circus, he prepared only rarely those horses belonging to *écuyers* and *écuyères* that asked him, and he pushed to *Haute École* only those of his own horses destined for the instruction of his *élite* students. His other training was limited to putting the horse in balance for outdoor work, to the re-establishment of his rectitude, to the development of his manageability in the natural gaits. They acquired a surety, an ease, a vigor, and a lightness that were no less striking than the perfection of his School work in the past.

It was to their training that he first applied his new means as he invented them. Afterward, he experimented with them, be it with his preferred students or again with confirmed old practitioners with an open mind, like Sainte-Reine. Their observations were added to those that Baucher himself made while watching them work. These observations formed the object of long meditations in his evenings because he lived very retired and had his only distraction in the daily game of checkers that he played at the Café de la Régence with his friend Gaussen.

Toward the end of the Empire, his health changed little by little. His injuries, from which he never ceased to suffer, often deprived him of sleep. He got heavy, and walking became so awfully hard that he had to get a cab to go to give his lessons. He rode only rarely and then only for a few moments to give a demonstration. His sight, which had never been excellent, weakened day by day and caused him unbearable headaches.

The defeat of our armies and the fall of the Empire struck him painfully, and the execution of General Clément Thomas by the *Communards* deprived him of a very dear friend whose fidelity had never failed.

Both of his eyes suffered from cataracts and only one could be operated on. From the end of 1871, he was nearly blind, and the year 1872 was not for him but a long aggravated suffering without end.

Deprived of the pension that the Emperor had given him and of the proceeds of his lessons, there remained only the strict necessities, that is when the frequent calls on his purse made by his son, whose life had not been exemplary, did not deprive him even of them.

At the beginning of 1873, he weakened rapidly, and saw death coming with serenity. General l'Hotte's piety has kept for us a recitation of his last days, and it is appropriate to leave here the words of the great Master's faithful disciple:

"I had been to see him on 28 February...

"On 7 March, I returned to Rue Amelot. I found Baucher in bed, his voice was less weak, it appeared to me to go a little bit better, but it was a deceptive better.

"He spoke to me of my regiment and again talked to me about his last technique. 'I have perhaps been able to succeed a little better than you,' he said to me, 'because I am more used to it, but I have seen, I have done it, and for sure, and it is the last word in equitation. The bridoon! *C'est si beau!'*

"Then taking my hand and giving it the position of the bridle hand, he said, 'Remember well: always this,' and he immobilized my hand under the pressure of his own. 'Never this,' and he brought my hand to my chest. 'I am happy to show you this again before dying.' Taking my leave, I embraced him and his hand tightened very affectionately on mine. I would not see him again except in his coffin.

"On the 11th, delirium seized him. Recognition came back only for moments. He was greatly agitated and distressed, but he got weaker, and he died during the night of 13 to 14 March at two o'clock in the morning."

So died at 78 years of age, a great artist and a perfectly "honest man" in the greatest extent of the sense that they gave to this term in the great century.

CHAPTER XI - BAUCHER'S SCHOOL

Baucher trained many students, and the number of them that became masters is surprising.

They in their turn explained his method in their writings, and for nearly all of them, these descriptive explanations differed notably from the text of the successive editions published by Baucher himself. All while proclaiming their otherwise incontestable fidelity to the principles of the Master, they brought modifications to his technique.

One of the most marked characteristics of the writings from the Baucher School is the variety of expression in the unity of the doctrine. This variety has causes, some coming from Baucher himself, others from his students.

We have seen above that the method never ceased to evolve during its author's whole career. There is no doubt that his teaching was submitted to a parallel evolution. In contrast, the text of the numerous successive editions remained the same, at least up until the 12th edition.[54] That is from where comes an evident reason for the divergences in the practice of the method that arose between the works of the Master and those of his students, but it is probably not the principal one.

It seems that it is also not in the "receptivity," if one could call it that, of these students that one has to look for the essential causes of the differences in interpretation that they gave to

---

54   From 1842 to 1864, the method came out in twelve editions, of which six were in the first two years. Baucher hardly had leave to revise his text and his contracts with the publishers permitted them to renew the publication whenever they wished.

the teaching that they had in common, and of which the base remained identical.

Baucher hardly ever instructed beginners in equitation. Nearly all of his students were already made riders before receiving his lessons, and their previous equestrian culture could not have failed to influence what they would take from their new instruction. Outside of some talented amateurs[55], Baucher's students were either professional civilian *écuyers* or officers.[56]

Among the former, whom Baucher called by the name in use at the time, "the professors of equitation," there were found *écuyers* from a high equestrian culture formed in the great schools of France and abroad, confirmed by an already long experience.

Baucher's military students were nearly all officers who were still young, but had followed at least one course at Saumur. The instruction that they had received there was probably limited to the use and training of the horse for military service and their experience was limited to the application of that training in their regiments. They were nonetheless already endowed with a solidly formative equestrian education.

The terrain of choice on which fell the Baucherist seed was therefore unequally prepared, and it was natural that its germination and its maturity were different.

All the same, the principal cause of modifications brought to the method's technique, as much by Baucher as by his students who became instructors in their turn, resided without any doubt in the difficulties encountered in the course of teaching it and putting it into practice.

For the horses, it was certainly because of the drawbacks that his students saw in the lowering of the neck that Baucher came to raise it. It was no less certainly from his students' difficulty in

---

55 Gaussen, Mackenzie-Grieves, Baron de Curnieu, etc.
56 It is curious to note that Baucher did not make any students of note in the Circus. The *écuyères* that presented his horses never got past that role and did not train any horses that appeared in public. Fillis perhaps should not be considered a direct student of Baucher and did not pretend otherwise.

obtaining the accord of the aides that he finished by excluding their simultaneous use as much as possible.

For the students become instructors, the difficulties in the transmission of the teaching were certainly greater yet, well that they were unequal for the civilians and the military.

The difficulties were formidable in the army, where equitation, as well as the training of horses, could only be practiced collectively in parades that were too large to allow continuity of individual observation, and that were composed of riders and horses that could only be called "all comers."

In the civilian *manèges*, beginners were often brought together in groups, but the Baucher method had nothing to do with elementary instruction that was intended to suffice for future "Sunday riders."

Those that aimed higher – and they have been numerous for over a hundred years (in 1948) – were necessarily a selection and they took private lessons from which they could benefit from their Master's constant control while putting his counsel into practice.

Also, everybody in the military had been directed to keep to a minimum their requirements from riders, as well as from horses, so as to reduce the tasks of both and, at the same time, to facilitate their proper control. The civilians were less bound by these considerations. Also they were nearly all content to point out the dangers of the abuse, more than the use, of the method's bold procedures without radically ruling them out. The military had to show themselves much more prudent.

Among the professionals, Lancosmes-Brèves[57] and Montigny[58] were the two most important because the evolution of their situations had put them in a position to teach, the first as the Master of the Manège in the largest establishment in Paris, the second as an *Écuyer* at Saumur and Pin, then as Inspector of the Dressage

---

57   The Comte de Lancosme-Brèves spent three years (1825 – 1828) as a student at the *Manège* des Pages under the direction of the Vicomte O'Hégerty, *Écuyer de Versailles*. He even appears to have followed for some time afterward the course for student *écuyers* at Versailles, directed by Comte d'Aure. Having joined the *Carabiniers* in 1829, he resigned in 1830. He again took lessons from d'Aure, this time at his civilian *manège* in Paris, and then with Baucher, of whom he rapidly became one of the most brilliant students.

Both were Baucherists "with reservations." It is not easy to clearly discern, according to their works, what they admit and what they reject of the method, but it is incontestable that what they adopted and professed was in the spirit of its author. Both of them pointed out the dangers of the abuse of the flexions and the spur. Lancosme-Brèves particularly made a point of these dangers, without however fixing the limits of the flexions and the spur, while Montigny more or less reduced the use of the flexions and prescribed the use of the whip, even of two whips, to prepare for, and in part, replace the use of the spur.

At first an ardent protagonist for the new method, he later had quarrels with Baucher where pride took precedence over doctrine. Savant horseman as much as skilled executor, he wanted to establish a theory of equitation on a basis of physiology and mechanics that was more exact than that of Baucher, which was, to truthfully say, quite fanciful. However his pretension to have founded a method that was his personally was not supportable because nothing essential distinguished it from that of Baucher.

Lancosme-Brèves directed the *Manège* Duphot in Paris from 1849 to 1864.

58   The Comte de Montigny was at first an officer in the Hussars in Hungary. Detached to the Spanish Riding School at the Vienna Court as a student, he became a *sous-écuyer*. Returning to France, he took lessons from d'Aure and then Baucher, with whom he stayed connected until the latter's death. He was an *écuyer* successively at the École d'État Major, then at the Haras, then at Saumur under the command of Comte d'Aure, and finally, until 1870, inspector of the Dressage Schools in the Administration des Haras (27 schools in 1868). He was the author of numerous works that were remarkable for the practical sense of their instructions.

Schools in the *Administration des Haras*. As to the depth and the principles of the method, it is yet more difficult to fix on what they thought. Lancosme-Brèves sharply criticized Baucher's theoretical demonstrations more than the propositions that they aimed to demonstrate. Montigny, whose works are not exempt from some contradictions, seems to have kept in the base of his training the seeking of a less horizontal position of the horse, a position more lifted in front than the position specified by Baucher in his First Manner, a position which however he later modified in the same direction as did Montigny.

It was again amongst the Baucherists "with reservations" that were lined up two skillful *écuyers* that taught in the *Manèges* of Paris, *de Sainte-Reine*[59] who insisted at length on the necessity to assure a good contact first before applying the flexions, and the *Vicomte Alexis d'Abzac*[60] who recommended the use of the gallop and strong contact alternated with the these same flexions.

Students of Baucher, civilians as much as military, who fully passed on the teaching that they had received without any suppression, addition, or attenuation, were few in number. These were all disciples of the last hour, and they incontestably constituted the *élite* of the School. The most eminent among them has been General Faverot de Kerbrech, but among the civilians, Rul and Lenoble du Teil described the Second Manner in works remarkable for their clarity, their simplicity, and their concision.

Rul had carefully followed Baucher's teaching from the beginning, but it is only the Second Manner that he described,

---

59   *Farmain de Sainte-Reine* (1803 – 1878) for seven years followed the lessons of the Ayrer brothers, celebrated Hannoverian *écuyers* at the *Manège* at the University of Göttingen. Afterwards he became *écuyer* to King Ernst August of Hannover, then to the King of Sardinia, and then taught at the School in Pignerolo. Returning to France around 1848, he took lessons from Baucher and remained his friend. He followed the whole evolution of the method and was one of the rare *écuyers* initiated into the Second Manner.

60   *Comte Alexis d'Abzac* belonged to the family of celebrated *Écuyers* of this name. He was still giving lessons at the *Manège* Pellier around 1885.

brilliantly, in his brochure on dressage that appeared in the last days of the Empire.

The work of Lenoble du Teil is more extended because he treats of both equitation and driving, but the part concerning dressage is equally simple, precise, and concise. This work appeared only in 1879.

In the Army, the method was widely used despite the interdiction to which it had been subjected by the Minister in 1842. This interdiction moreover had been written in a peculiar way and applied only to equitation. At the same time that it was formulated, there appeared an official brochure entitled, "New Method, *approved by the Minister*, for training young horses according to the principles of Monsieur Baucher."

In the shelter of this approbation, Commandant de Novital, *Écuyer* en Chef at Saumur, had introduced the method at the School with all the passion that he put into everything.

After de Novital, the excellent results obtained by Comte d'Aure well justified the preference of the Cavalry Committee for his method, but they did not stop the propagation of Baucher's method in the regiments, or even in the School.

After the departure of d'Aure, a whole host of *Écuyers* and *Sous-Maîtres* who had had the good fortune to study both methods, even in the most favorable conditions at the School, did their best to combine them so as to benefit from their advantages while avoiding their drawbacks.

For nine years, Commandant Guérin, successor to Comte d'Aure at the head of the *Manège*, was the most ardent partisan and the most skillful artisan of this "fusion" where Baucherism played a more than large part.

On the other hand, Commandant l'Hotte, who after Guérin took on the direction of the *Manège* from 1864 to 1870, proscribed the Baucher method, as he was to do again as General Commandant of the School from 1874 to 1879. A strong widespread legend makes of the General a martyr to discipline: that he had sacrificed his convictions out of military duty and obeyed the ministerial interdiction that struck at the method of which he was a partisan. But the General has written (*Un Officier de Cavalerie*, p. 246 (*A Cavalry Officer*)), "According to whether campaign or scholarly equitation is envisioned, the preference must be given to the principles of d'Aure or those of Baucher." This declaration, so clear, cannot leave any doubt about the conformity of his personal opinion with that of his leadership at the Cavalry School. But even under his command, the generation of "Fusionnaires" (those who combined the two schools) still populated the *Manège*, and until he left in 1876, Commandant Dutilh, *Écuyer en Chef*, would not forget all that he had learned as *Sous-Maître* and *Sous-Écuyer* under Commandant Guérin, so his teaching remained strongly tinted by Baucherism.

In the regiments, the Baucherists were numerous, and many of them became *écuyers* of great merit.

After 1845, Captain Raabe showed everybody that, in the application of the method, one could use the whip to avoid the dangers of the spur. After him, Gerhardt, Wachter, and many others reduced the danger even more by simplifying this preparation, and one could say that Gerhardt developed a very practical Military Baucherism that Bonie later could only copy.

So, at the end of the Empire, well that its interdiction had never been lifted, Baucher's method had numerous adept and distinguished representatives in the Army, just as in the world of civilian riders.

But it was a subdued Baucherism. Even if its principles never varied, its practice, judiciously modified, had nothing of the heroic era.

These modifications had been brought to the practice either by Baucher's students or by Baucher himself.

His students, following Raabe, had above all developed the use of the whip, and accordingly, reduced the difficulties in the use of the spur. They had also reduced the difficulties in the use of the flexions that Gerhardt was later even to abandon.

Baucher himself made more changes. He formulated the rule "Hand without legs, legs without hand" that avoided their too often inevitable disaccord. He replaced the lowering of the neck by its lifting so as to shorten the arm of the lever that is the neck, which gave the horse a position that is much closer to that which he takes up at liberty and that frees up his gaits.

That is of what the Second Manner precisely consists. Unfortunately it remained nearly unknown for lack of publicity and because certain of those adept at the First Manner had not been able or had not wanted to study the Second Manner, pretending even to see in it a renunciation of "principles" that it did not really entail in any fashion.

In fact, it was with the Empire, especially between 1860 and 1870 that the new School found its golden age.

The dressage establishments of the Administration des Haras were Baucherised by Montigny. The civilian *manèges* were not less so in Paris with the Pelliers, father and son, and with Lancosme-Brèves himself, despite his quarrels with Baucher; in the provinces with Rul at the *Manège* at Reims, Ducas at Bordeaux, Caron at Douai, etc., etc....

In the Army, the success was yet more complete.

The whole Cavalry Division of the Guard practiced the method. Its Commander, General Morris, a brilliant rider and remarkable horseman, was a resolute partisan. The Captain Instructors, Gerhardt in the Lancers, Daudel in the *Chausseurs*, de Lioux in the Guides, Michel in the Horse Artillery Regiment, obtained incontestable results. Commandant Guérin at the Cavalry School, like Commandant Digeon at the École d'État Major, then at St-Cyr, were convinced Baucherists, and at the School at Saumur, during the d'Aurist reaction by General l'Hotte, Baucherism found refuge in the Cadre Bleu, where Captain Gerhardt, promoted to *Chef d'Escadrons*, (squadron leader) had been named Chief Instructor for Military Exercises.

In the provincial garrisons, the 5th Dragoons still carried the imprint of Captain Raabe who had retired in 1861. Wachter evangelized the 7th *Cuirassiers*, Teulières the 8th *Chasseurs*, and Bonie the regiments in Lyon, etc., etc....

The minister let sleep the interdiction, going back 25 years, that had struck the method, and practiced "fusion" in giving, on the one hand, official consecration to Comte d'Aure's course of equitation, and in buying, on the other hand, in 1867, "*Méthode d'Équitation et de Dressage Presentée par Monsieur Rul à Saumur, et Approvée par le Conseil d'Instruction de l'École*" (*Method of Equitation and Dressage Presented by Monsieur Rul at Saumur, and Approved by the Instruction Council of the School*). Yet, Rul was the most fanatic of Baucher's students...

The Emperor himself "fused" his own manner. After the formation of the *Cent-Gardes* in 1854, he charged Baucher with putting on a course for them at Saint-Cloud. Close to the same time, d'Aure was named Inspector of the Imperial Stables, then *Écuyer* to the Emperor, then Inspector-General of the Studs. Finally, after Comte d'Aure's death, the Emperor, from his own purse, accorded Baucher an unsolicited pension.

After 1870, Baucherism lost ground. Political influence, which had at first aided the flowering of his popularity twenty-five years earlier, only to clash with it as time went by, was no stranger to his decline.

Baucher, pensioner of the Empire, and Commandant Faverot de Kerbrech, former Aide-de-Camp to Napoleon III, were suspect to the republicans, who also saw without pleasure The Comte de Montigny, ousted from the Studs, keep his imperial beard and his waxed mustache. The Bauchérists were labeled as part of the Bonapartist bloc. General l'Hotte, not content to proscribe the method from the School at Saumur, gave it a yet more severe blow by writing, himself, in pure d'Aurist orthodoxy, the Instructions for Riding in the Regulation of 1876 for the Cavalry.

However, for a long time the preparation of the horse on whip continued to be practiced in the Division at Lyon, passed on from the Command of General Bonie, and in the Régiment de Chausseurs, from Colonel Chaverondier, just as in all the units where there remained any of the *"fusionnaires"* until retirement little by little eventually eliminated them.

The "Father," Raabe, despite his age, still taught, but the best of his military students, Commandant Bonnal, belonging to the Infantry, was badly placed for propagating his method. The last students of Baucher were in full maturity, but few among them were in the Army. Colonel Faverot de Kerbrech, after a mission to America that allowed him to be forgotten, explained well the "Last Teachings of Baucher" to the cadres of his regiment when he took command of the 28th Dragoons at Meaux, but the Inspection of Remounts, the position that he next occupied for the ten years until his death, was a situation unfavorable to disseminating the Baucherist doctrine.

Henri Baucher, the son, gave a few courses to the officers in the garrisons at St-Etienne, Bordeaux, Montpellier, Fontainbleau, etc.... But they were courses comprising only thirty group lessons. What is more, crippled with rheumatism, the teacher no longer rode, except with the greatest of difficulty, and for lack of being able to join the example with the precepts, the results that he obtained were quite thin.

Finally, sportive equitation, after quite some difficulty, penetrated the army, and military competitions developed widely.[61] Provided that he would be keen and *"fin prêt,"* (ready) it was of little importance that a horse be very easy to handle in order to succeed in sports, and his sports training would take precedence over his dressage.

In the world of civilian riders, the method resisted better. Lenoble du Teil taught at Pin until 1898. Barroil, a student of Raabe, in 1887 wrote the equestrian testament of his Master,

---

61   The ministerial fluctuations were no less marked with regard to competitions than they were in the matter of equestrian methods. In 1856, competitions had been forbidden to officers, and the ban was renewed in 1857. But the Minister attended those at Saumur in person in 1859. In 1863, the ban was lifted for some six steeplechases. In 1868, there was a new formal ban, confirmed in 1869: "since their introduction into the Army, military competitions have not resulted in any equestrian improvement in the officers."

who would go on to form more students, amateur and professional, like Gastines, Auguste Raux, and Desurmont up to 1889.

Around 1890, there appeared one after the other *"Principes de Dressage et d'Équitation"* by Fillis (See James Fillis, *Breaking and Riding*, Lyons Press, Guilford CT, 2005), *"L'Équitation Diagonale"* (*Diagonal Equitation*) by Captain J. B. Dumas, and *"L'Équitation Actuelle"* (*Equitation Today*) by Doctor Lebon.

Their authors were not completely Baucherists but they were still *"Bauchérisants."* All three, in recognizing without beating around the bush the value and scope of Baucher's method, severely condemned the curling of the neck, already abandoned by Baucher himself in 1867, and presented as a discovery, of which Fillis attributed the paternity to himself, the lifting of the neck, prescribed by Baucher more than thirty years earlier!

Their excuse was, as has been said above, the obscurity in which remained the Second Manner, which did not receive its definite expression until the remarkable work of General Faverot de Kerbrech, published only in 1891. (*Methodical Dressage of the Riding Horse*, Xenophon Press 2010)

Fillis left few students in France, J.-B. Dumas and Lebon even less.

With the passage of time, the Masters of *Manège* and their *écuyers*, *Bauchérists* or *Bauchérisants* disappeared little by little. They were replaced most often by former *Sous-Maîtres* from the Military Schools whose training carried less and less trace of Baucherism.

Moreover in France, fewer and fewer saddle horses were trained, and the brochure, *"à Hue et à Dia"* (*Gee and Haw*) by Commandant Blacque-Belair was aimed at civilians as well as the military.

Outside of France, the success of the new method had been at first very keen, but it hardly lasted.

It was, as soon as it appeared, translated into all the languages of Europe, but the translations surely did not make it clearer for the riders who attempted to apply it with the book as their only guide. Without a doubt did they experience the same setbacks as their colleagues in France.

Baucher's artistic tours and his somewhat prolonged stays in Berlin permitted him to show and demonstrate what he had explained in writing. Consequently, the results were such that the craze for his method died only after rigorous official pressure, which it could not survive despite the efforts of Rul, who traveled all over Europe to spread the new gospel, but without great success.

At Vienna, the secular authority of the Court Spanish Riding School was too well ensconced to be shaken. A few personalities, like the famous Count Sandor, took lessons from Baucher, but it was a success without a future.

In Italy, where Baucher had kept up relations in the world of professionals dating from his youth, the method was quite welcomed and even adopted in the Court of Naples, but it does not appear to have survived the fall of François II.

In Russia, François Caron, a student of Baucher, served at the Court for a long time as *Écuyer* to the Tsar, and the nomination of his student Fillis to the Cavalry School at Saint Petersburg as *Écuyer en Chef* in 1898 was probably due to the persistence of his memory.

In Belgium, the Baucherist influence lasted longer, despite the opposition of the partisans of German equitation, like Brochkowski and Van der Meer. It was maintained by apostolic visits by Rul, and still persisted in 1887, when Captain Van der Hove published a paraphrasing of Gerardt's "Manuel," and applied it with success to many Cavalry Regiments. In the meanwhile as well, Fillis gave lessons to the Guides in Brussels.

In England, Henri Baucher formed several students. But the best one, Parr, came back to teach in Paris. The English did not feel the need to train their horses: when the horses did not train themselves, they were simply sold off in France.

Baucher's school remained very united.

Only Lancosme-Brèves claimed the paternity of a supposedly reformed method, but it was not distinguished from that of the Master by anything essential, nor anything original, and no one followed him in his schism.

The use of auxiliary means, as with that of the whip, certainly provoked some quarrels in the School. They were all brought up by Gerhardt whether against his colleagues or against Baucher himself, who however, General l'Hotte tells us, "had tried everything."

Those students of the First Manner who renounced it to adopt the Second Manner were little numerous for lack of knowledge of the Second Manner. Gerhardt, who did not know anything about it, was the only one to attack it and went all the way to writing, "Then Baucher is no longer Baucher."

The *Bauchérisants* like Fillis and Dumas were further from the communion of the faithful, and one could hardly reproach them, they were writing 70 years after the appearance of the method, and the "Last Teachings," [*Methodical Dressage of the Riding Horse...*, Xenophon Press 2010] handed down by General Faverot de Kerbrech, had not yet appeared! One should not therefore apply to them the affront that Rul landed on Lancosme-Brèves: "Again one... who cut himself a 'doublet from the King's coat.'"

CHAPTER XII – AND NOW?

And now, what remains of *"Bauchérisme?"* In appearance, not much, in reality, much more than is generally believed.

For soon to be forty years (in 1948), in France, the Army has been redoing Baucherism without knowing it. Since the reduction of military service from five to three years, and even before, it had become evident that the equitation from the 1876 Regulation was too difficult for the men of the troop. Faced with the impossibility of getting the rider of the ranks to "accord" his aids, the Cavalry Command endeavored to avoid the occasions of their disaccord by prescribing the avoidance of their simultaneous use as much as possible; so well did they do so that around 1912, the "formula: 'legs without hands, hands without legs'" became the fundamental rule of our military equitation.

Some members of the Cavalry Committee of that time knew perhaps that this formula was more than thirty years old, but the Commission did not believe it had to render unto Caesar what was his by designating its author by name.

One could object that equitation without legs had always been practiced by a great many bad riders, but the great majority of our horses fortunately have enough natural impulsion to only need rare use of impulsive aids. "Hand without legs," even deprived of its counterpart, is still therefore a formula of which the application remains infinitely less dangerous than that of *"Tirez-dessus – Tapez-dedans"* (push and pull) that almost infallibly resulted in the fruitless search for the famous "accord of the aids."

On the other hand, one peculiarity that is perhaps much more characteristic of current French equitation is the generalized use of the counter rein of pressure (the neck rein) to obtain a turn.

The *anciens* were not ignorant of it but they hardly ever practiced it. Monfaucon, the only *écuyer* from Versailles who ever wrote anything, did not even mention it. Outside of France, the cavalries that had not been subjected to the influence of Baucher barely began to use it in 1914 and their regulations still prescribed the most complicated contortions of the wrist to permit the left hand, holding all four reins, to make the right reins act as direct reins.

And yet it was again Baucher who regularized, even systematized, and vulgarized the turn on the counter rein. d'Aure explained its effect well, but he only prescribed its use in combination with the direct rein, which brought up difficulties in their "accord."

The French of today (1948), who so habitually use, sometimes all the way to abuse, the unique effect of the counter rein of pressure for turning, also act according to Baucherism without knowing it.

The gentlemen who, in the entryway to the arena, administer a last whack of the whip to their horse before entering, do they know that this procedure is an "invention" by Baucher?

Outside of the Army, we encounter among the few professionals, and the rare amateurs who go beyond elementary dressage, riders who recommend themselves to Baucher with qualifications that are a bit light to justify this pretension.

Using in dressage, as they nearly all do, the rotation of the croup around the shoulders, for example, they separate themselves in effect from the method of only the general suppling of the whole horse as practiced by the Old Masters, and abandon the practice then to adopt the localization of a partial suppling inserted into a series of exercises applied separately to all parts of the horse successively. This momentary localization of supplings is surely in effect one of the characteristics of Baucher's method, but it is not the *essential* characteristic, which consists of the *mise en main*, that is to say, the flexibility of the jaw in the *ramener* that alone permits the horse to execute his work "as if by himself."

But the horses of these pretend Baucherists remain most often outside of the *mise en main*.

Some of them certainly have the neck and head fixed in an position close to the *ramener*, but the mouth, supported more or less inflexibly on the hand, remains mute, whether by inertia or by contraction. The position so imposed on the front end very much facilitates the gaits of fantasy based on the *'jambette"* that these riders practice exclusively. They call a sort of Spanish trot a "passage" that does not lack brilliance, but remains precipitated, convulsive, and cannot be "melted" into the piaffe, the execution of which remains precluded for them.

Others arrive at more varied results, but all of their school airs are executed with the horse in a position that does not permit complete development of the airs. The necessary lightening of the forehand results, nearly exclusively for their horses, from the lifting of the upper half of the neck without the *ramener* being sufficient to re-establish the top-line in all its suppleness, nor to assure to the efforts of the hindquarters all their capacity in the lifting of the mass of the body.

The lightness of these horses is hardly but a reduction in their contact coming at the same time from the shortening of the front end and the limitation of the efforts of the hindquarters, without a useful *rassembler*.

This is therefore how, under another form, again from the lack of a *mise en main*, these riders are separated from what is essential in Baucher's method. So in our day we encounter on the one hand a great many riders that are Baucherists who do not know it, and on the other hand, some riders who believe that they are Baucherists but are much less so than they think.

Finally, for more than thirty years, international competitions in dressage have put in front of our champions problems so difficult to resolve that the teaching in our military schools, always more or less d'Aurist, often furnishes proof of its inadequacy outside of daily equitation.

The rare examples of the "Last Teaching of Baucher", of which the only edition is out of print, have been so actively sought that their market value has increased tenfold.

The last revenge of the artistic Master of Equitation on the equitation of the outdoors...

Baucher riding Capitaine: short stop at the gallop.

APPENDIX I – EXCERPT FROM THE MEMOIR OF EUGÈNE CARON AND LOUIS RUL

Written by E. Caron

THE 3ᴿᴰ LANCERS IN 1842

At the beginning of the year 1842, the 3ʳᵈ Lancers had held the garrison in Paris for nearly a year. The district called *"de Sens"* had been allocated to it "provisionally" upon its arrival, but the provision lasted still.

The regiment comprehended but three squadrons, probably by reason of the weakness of its effective strength in horses and of *Service de Place* by "made up squadrons" that was in vigor in Paris.

The morale of the regiment was mediocre, at least in the ranks. The core of *sous-officiers* was contaminated by politics. A great many of them were or had been *Carbonari*.[62] The majority had been Bonapartists since the landing at Boulogne. An epidemic of duels ravaged the garrison. The troopers were malcontented with the service, which consisted only of being continually on guard or on patrol, on horse or on foot. The incessant wearing of full dress for this service ruined the "individual masses" and the men grumbled bitterly. They consoled themselves by accepting the too numerous invitations to drink

---

62   Italian: lit. "charcoal-burners", the name of secret societies of a revolutionary tendency which played an active part in the history of Italy and France early in the 19th century

from "suspicious individuals" and cases of drunkenness were so numerous that the night patrols were followed by a van to bring the dead-drunk lancers back to the district.

No instruction was given in the regiment, except for some "squadron schools" the day before reviews that were somewhat frequent. The recruits did not join up with the corps until after having finished their classes at the Depot at Libourne, where they had stayed from eight to twelve months. The men did not see their officers except on occasions of administrative service and hardly knew them.

The effective strength of horses did not reach 300 for an effective strength of more than 450 men. Only the officers had assigned horses. The remount for the regiment was quite disparate. The numerous aged horses all came from the South, where the regiment had been garrisoned for a long time. The others were of diverse provenance and models. Since the arrival of the regiment in Paris, they had been remounted only from the Purchasing Depot at Valenciennes. The sources for this depot were German merchants installed in Belgium, and their horses came for the most part from Hungary. Only a few of these horses were really young, and those that were available were so few that the purchasing officer often bought some whose mouths had been visibly refreshed. Incidentally, these horses did give satisfaction and cost between 300 to 500 francs.

According to regulations, the horses for the remount first had to be attached to the regiment's depot, which was charged with their training, and were not to be delivered to the corps until a year later. They were to be divided among the squadrons with the exception of a reserve called the "Little Remount," placed under the orders of a Captain Instructor, and destined to make up for unexpected falls in the effective strength of the squadrons. The state of health was very bad. Periodic disease reigned continually. A great many horse were declared unfit by reason of blindness. The forage was very bad and the rations quite insufficient. In the District of Sens, the pumps were frequently dry, and the water for horses was deplorable.

Since the 3rd Lancers had been in Paris, the horses' stay in the remount at the Depot in Libourne for their training had been done away with because of the distance from the Depot, the crushing requirements of *Service de Place*, and the weakness in the effective strength of horses. As soon as the Purchasing Depot announced the collection of about twenty horses assigned to the regiment, a mounted detachment was immediately sent from the *Corps* to Valenciennes to take delivery of the lot and bring it directly to Paris. The horses that were shown to be the more docile on the trip were assigned to a squadron as soon as they arrived, and the others to the Little Remount. The latter however presented little difficulty in general and then almost only because of their "fearful character" and the frights that they experienced in the city, probably by reason of their bad eyesight.

MARÉCHAL DES LOGIS CARON

In 1842, Eugène Jacques Caron, son of a battalion commander in the Grand Army was *Maréchal des Logis* for the 3rd Lancers. He was thirty years old and had 12 years of service. He was ending his second "leave" in 7 years, over the course of which he had spent a number of years at the Regimental Depot at Libourne, where he had been constantly employed in the training of young horses. Since his return to the Corps in 1840, he had been assigned to the Little Remount.

His employment was greatly envied because his posting and seniority exempted him from the greater part of *Service de Place*, and also because the Captain Instructor, Monsieur de Mésange, as well as his assistant, Lieutenant de Scée, were very well liked by the troops. Furthermore, the *sous-officier* of the Little Remount had the privilege of leading the detachments sent to Valenciennes to pick up the young horses. During the trip, which could last more than a month, the Lancers were frequently invited to their hosts' tables at the stage stops. They therefore realized some economies on their slim indemnity for the road and returned to Paris with a good provision of contraband tobacco.

The last trip had been made at the beginning of the winter of 1841 – 1842 and the convoy that had been gathered was larger than customary. Besides the horses assigned to the regiment, it included a group of horses destined to the Cavalry School. The Régiment de Chasseurs in Orléans was supposed to take this lot on from Paris to Saumur, but because many cases of farcin[63] had been declared at Orléans, the departure of the detachment that was supposed to come to take over these horses in Paris had been deferred and it had not yet been accomplished by the month of March. Horses destined for Saumur had remained on subsistence at the Little Remount, and the lot had to be completed by a certain number of horses furnished by the 3rd Lancers, despite its poverty. They were destined, according to the orders, to troop service in the instruction squadrons at the School, and one of them had to be "of grey coat" to be assigned to the Trumpet School.

In the Regiment, there was precisely one grey horse from the south, badly castrated, that the squadrons passed on each time that they found the occasion to get rid of him because he was "poison in the stable." He was a biter, struck out in front, and refused to be bridled. Once mounted, he was not stubborn, not even difficult, but he bit his neighbors in the ranks, carrying on with veritable roaring, and he reared in the presence of mares. He was quite naturally designated for the Trumpet School at Saumur.

During the month of March, Caron was warned by Captain de Mésange that 16 horses from the Little Remount would shortly be used for an experiment in a new system of training invented by a civilian *écuyer* named Baucher, of whom the Captain spoke very well.

They also knew from the secretaries in the Report Room that the regiment had received an order to furnish fifty horses for these experiments. The Colonel had observed that the Regiment's service should consequently be reduced, but the Paris Headquarters was opposed, and the number of horses was reduced by half. Each squadron then received an order to designate "four

---

63   A contagious disease

horses, including one belonging to a rank and mounted by him. The others, of which 'at least one will be chosen from amongst those presenting difficulties,' would be mounted by older and vigorous riders *(sic)*."

The experience from that perspective, naturally received a lot of comments in the Regiment. According to general opinion, it amounted to a type of taming in which the fights necessitated all the vigor called for by the memorandum, and the designated Lancers showed a great deal of pride, tempered by no anxiety.

Caron did not know any more than the others and it seems that at that time he had never attended any of Baucher's performances at the *Cirque des Champs Élysées*. However, he had heard of the *écuyer* from one of the riders in the Little Remount, named Vallin, son of a horse dealer in Paris, and who had been a stable boy at the *Manège Pellier* where Baucher trained his horses. Vallin recounted extraordinary stories about Monsieur Baucher and his dressage, but he was a braggart that no one took seriously.

At that time, the horses in the Little Remount were all of docile character. Only a few showed fear and like a great many Hungarian horses "did not have clear eyes." All of them had already been ridden in the double bridle and many of them in complete tack and harness trappings with sabre and lance. All of the training that they had received consisted of walking them in the city to habituate them to the movement in the street.

Maréchal des Logis Caron therefore awaited these experiments with curiosity and without worry.

THE EXPERIENCE OF THE BAUCHER METHOD

The first sessions of training announced for the 15th were put back several times. Finally on the 20th, Caron received the order to present the next day at the *manège*, at a time not indicated, only two horses. The squadrons did not present any horses that day. It had been Monsieur Baucher, said Captain de Mésange, who had requested the adoption of this manner of doing things so that the riders receiving instruction on the first day could be used afterwards as monitors, and their horses as models.

Two horses were designated by the Captain Instructor on the recommendation of Caron who would ride one of them while the other would be ridden by Vallin, the trooper who claimed to know Baucher.

The next day, at the prescribed hour, Caron and Vallin were waiting in the *manège* at their horses' heads. They were surprised to be joined by two horses from the 5th Cuirassiers ridden by *sous-officiers*. Recent duels had taken place between the *sous-officiers* of the two regiments between which the rapport was hardly cordial. The two groups, dismounted, acted as if they did not see each other.

At the door of the *manège*, some officers circled another officer whose "blue black" uniform greatly intrigued the troopers. Caron who had previously driven horses from Libourne to Saumur, recognized this officer as an *écuyer* from the Cavalry School.

Monsieur Baucher arrived late and tipped his hat without excusing himself. He was accompanied by a young man with a dark complexion that he presented to the officers without the riders being able to hear his name. Monsieur Baucher called the two groups of riders to the middle of the *manège*, where they stood facing one another so that Baucher himself and his companion stood between them. The *Écuyer* from Saumur, as well as Captain de Mésange and a Captain from the 5th Cuirassiers approached them while the other officers stayed at the end of the *manège*. M. Baucher began to speak and said: "the horse's disobediences to the reins come from his raising his head when the rider uses the reins," and the horse refuses to turn to the side "of the rein that is used." To make him docile to the reins, one must therefore teach him to keep his head low, and to bend his neck to the indicated side. "He spoke in a conversational tone without 'full sentences' *(sic)*.

Then taking one of the cavalry horses himself, M. Baucher showed them what he called "the three flexions" while his aide did the same on one of the lancer horses.

- Lateral flexion on the curb bit, the reins held *under* the neck.
- Flexion of lowering of the neck.

- Lateral flexion on the bridoon, the rein used passing *over* the neck, and turning it.

While acting on the reins, M. Baucher explained how the force employed must be slow and continuous as long as the horse resists it, reduced as soon as he yields, and retaken until the head is brought little by little to the position "to the right or to the left" for the lateral flexions and until the level of the knees in the lowering.

M. Baucher always spoke very clearly and demonstrated what he wanted to say by doing it at the same time as he said it.

The cavalry horse did not bend easily to the side because his neck was short and thick, while the lancer horse turned his head with the greatest facility. It was the inverse for the lowering of the neck: the cavalry horse only had to be asked to execute it, while the lancer horse fought against the hand. After several minutes both horses obeyed willingly, then M. Baucher and his aide took on the other two horses. The second cavalry resisted by backing up, and M. Baucher, without trying to stop him, followed him step by step all the way to the wall, where he decided to yield. The lancer yielded so easily "that one could have believed that he already knew the lesson."

Then M. Baucher had the flexions executed by the riders themselves. He helped the cavalrymen and his companion helped the lancers. Each one of them held, in his own hands, the hands of the rider while the rider acted on the reins. He insisted on the giving and retaking of the hand following submission or resistance, on the necessity of being content with little, and on the importance of caresses as soon as willingness manifested itself.

In brief, in about twenty minutes, the four horses frankly turned their heads to the right and to the left, without lifting them, on the action of each of the four reins.

M. Baucher then had the riders mount their horses to have them repeat the flexions from the saddle, first on the bridoon, then on the curb, with the horse remaining at the halt. He and his aide, after having brought them under the neck, took the pair of reins not used by the rider and used them to prevent the horses from lifting their heads, but only when the horse tried to do it. M. Baucher did not have the lowering of the head executed directly by the riders, not alone, nor with his help or that of his assistant. He then told them to take a bridoon rein in each hand, the curb reins abandoned on the horse's neck, and promenade their horses in all directions in the *manège* at the walk, and gradually turn more tightly. In fact, the horses turned with the greatest facility. But, said Caron: "the Hungarians have never presented difficulty in doing so." The whole process had lasted about half an hour.

After several minutes of work at will, M. Baucher brought the four riders together around him without making them dismount and resumed his instruction, still being very familiar.

"You have seen," he told them, "how much the flexions improve the guiding of the horse and make the turns easy. However, the flexions can only facilitate them; the flexions do not permit forcing the horse to turn. That comes from making the horse turn like a wheelbarrow pushed by a man: for the wheelbarrow to turn to the right, it would be absolutely necessary for the man who is pushing it to turn himself at first to the left until the wheelbarrow turns to the new direction. For the horse, it is the hind legs that push him, like the man does for the wheelbarrow between the shafts. For the horse to be obliged to turn to the right, one must be able to force his hindquarters to move from right to left. The right rein alone does not suffice when the horse resists. It requires the aid of the right leg, and often even the spur. The same as we made 'the flexion of the shoulders' (*sic*), we are going to apply to the horse 'the flexion of the haunches.'"

He then ordered Caron, who found himself the closest to Baucher, to adjust the bridoon a little taut, and to progressively close the left leg. Baucher himself had seized the left rein next to the ring. The horse, a little worried, pressed against the leg while twisting his tail. Then M. Baucher told Caron to apply the spur frankly, and, at the same time, vigorously drew to the left the head of the horse who decided to move his haunches to the right. "The spur must stop its pressure immediately," said M. Baucher, caressing the horse for a long time. After two or three repetitions of this flexion, M. Baucher had Caron execute the same work with the right leg, Baucher himself holding the right rein. His aide proceeded the same way with the two cavalry horses, and M. Baucher with the second lancer horse. Finally M. Baucher told the four riders to make, at his command, a right face and a left face. After some interventions by M. Baucher and his aide by means of the rein on the same side as the leg employed, but only for the less docile horses, all four "obeyed properly" on just the action of their riders. M. Baucher then had them dismount, and before terminating the lesson, he reviewed it in nearly the same terms as over the course of the instruction: "The flexion of the shoulders makes the turn easy, but it is the flexion of the haunches that imposes it." Of course, added M. Baucher, we have only outlined the work that has to be perfected by exercise, the same as it is necessary to repeat weapons drill to make it lively and precise.

The following session was more eventful. A squadron was designated to provide two new horses, and the cavalry riders also brought out two more. One of those from the lancers was the grey destined for the Trumpets at Saumur. When his rider, who lacked assurance, made a motion to flex him, the horse wanted only to bite him. M. Baucher took the horse himself, approaching him at the level of his saddle. He adroitly seized the left rein towards the middle of the rein, holding the right rein tightly, he then nimbly slid his left hand along the left rein to hold it firmly by the curb rein ring. The strong tension on the right rein prevented the horse from turning his head to the left to bite. Then he began to "roar" and tried to strike out in front, but M. Baucher was too close to the shoulder and behind it for the horse to strike him. Then M. Baucher, firmly holding both reins, forced him to back up quickly. The horse tried hard to rear, but M. Baucher then tightened the right rein as much as it would go and the torsion on the horse's neck made him immediately fall back to the ground. All the riders had naturally stopped occupying themselves with their own horses and followed the peripatetic[64] fight, but M. Baucher, who showed the greatest calm and the most perfect ease, told his aide to give the lesson to the new arrivals, who did not present any difficulty.

---

64   Traveling on foot.

All the while flexing their horses, the riders nonetheless continued to observe M. Baucher, who made the horse back up in all directions more and more rapidly despite the horse's cries and his striking out into a void. The battle lasted a good quarter of an hour, at the end of which the horse gave in, trembling in all his legs, white with foam, camped out, head low, and let his neck be flexed by M. Baucher, who still kept his position near the shoulder. M. Baucher then called Caron, made him mount the horse, and move right away to the lesson of the legs, against which the horse did not defend himself at all. After some flexions of the haunches to the right and left that the horse executed easily, M. Baucher told Caron to walk at will in the *manège* avoiding passing too close to the other horses. "The horse appeared struck with stupor."

To some degree, this incident had caused trouble for the execution of the second lesson, in the course of which M. Baucher at first repeated the explanations of the day before for the newcomers, while the "experienced riders" executed the flexions at the same time as he described them. Then while the new riders executed the exercise in their turn under the directions of the aide, the "experienced riders" received from M. Baucher the lesson of the "rein back one step," finished by the repetition of the work at the walk from the day before, with "turns in all directions," executed finally at the collected trot with "the reins held short."

Caron continues to describe, in the greatest detail, the remainder of Baucher's lessons.

Their progression consisted of:

- **Work at the walk and the trot** on a single track in the *ramener*. Baucher did not, other than accidentally speak of relaxation of the jaw. He did not use the expression *"mise en main."* His only constant demand was the pronounced flexion of the poll. (These observations were not made until afterwards when many years later Caron again took lessons from Baucher and took note of modifications to his teaching.)
- **Pirouettes on the hindquarters, executed** step by step as had been the pirouettes on the forehand before.

- **Rein back,** on which Baucher insisted a great deal. Caron observed that certain horses rapidly began to rein back too quickly and too easily.
- *Effet d'ensemble.* The progression is very slow and very prudent. It comported at first the request, alternating and prolonged, of departs from the halt on the action of the legs and the spur, and the rein back on the action of the reins only, also from the halt. It was only after a long sequence of these alternating requests that immobility was sought on the combined and simultaneous action of the legs and hand, employed at first each with the greatest moderation, then with a progressively increased force, but always equivalent. When, at the end of the procedure, the leg aid increased up to the pressure of the spur, a depart from the halt forward finished the *effet d'ensemble* when the hand "opened the barrier" and the legs persisted in their action, or augmented it to activate the depart.
- **Work on two tracks,** at the walk and at the trot. It was reduced to "half a haunches-in with the head to the wall" executed only along the long walls of the *manège*.
- **Depart at the canter.** Baucher gave it his full attention. With the *ramener*, it seemed that this was the principal object of his lessons. It was to be requested on a circle, but after a half-turn on the haunches outside of the circle. The horse being on a circle to the left, half-turn on the haunches to the right, and depart at the canter to the right on a circle to the right.

Finally, after 26 lessons, the horses were presented to the General in parades of 10, because of the dimensions of the *manège*. Complete tack, sabre and lance. The parade was done almost entirely at the canter. It comprehended successive movements, circles and changes of circle. For the change of circle, the horses passed through the trot and the flying change was not sought, but "nearly all the Hungarian horses did it on their own." The cavalry horses were heavier and took up the new canter with difficulty, even though their riders rode with two hands.

For individual movements, with the riders being numbered 1's and 2's, the number 2's left the track on command, and placed themselves either at the side of their number 1, or in front of him. Same work for the number 1's. Then individual pairs halted short and prolonged on the centre line, followed by depart at the walk, change of hand, and depart at the canter when reaching the track. On the whole, "all the parades went very well," said Caron.

It was not until later that Caron, on the point of setting up a *manège* at Douai, took an individual course from Baucher where the Master taught him to execute the flexions of the jaw before those of the neck.

This detail well confirms this passage that one can read in the text of the method:

"...In principle, I felt, despite the flexibility of the neck, resistances for which I was not able to determine the cause. The followers of my method, to whom I have not had the occasion to make known the new procedure that I have come to explain, will learn with pleasure that, all in perfecting the suppling of the forehand, this procedure, by completing it, saves a great economy of time...."

So it was that the method "with continuous creation" never ceased to be perfected by its author.

The General warmly congratulated Baucher and his aide and expressed his satisfaction to the troops, whom he exempted from guard duty for a month. After the General's departure, Captain de Mésange gave a lance blade embroidered in silk to Baucher for a souvenir. "The *Cuirasssiers*, who had not been warned, had nothing to offer and "were vexed."

CARON AT SAUMUR

On 20 March, Caron set out for Saumur at the head of a detachment of horses assigned to the School. He rode the grey destined for the trumpets and cared for the horse himself throughout the journey. Arriving at Saumur, the horse was "very settled down." He let himself be bandaged, saddled, and bridled without striking out or biting, but he was "always crying out."

At Saumur, where he arrived on 19 April, the Maréchal des Logis was recognized by Commandant de Novital, who made him ride his grey horse in front of the parade of *Sous-Officiers* from the cadre.

Very embarrassed by his role, Caron executed a certain number of movements at the command of the *Écuyer en Chef*. "That went mediocrely," he wrote, but the parade of *Sous-Officiers* "was yet more mediocre and even bad... A rain of kicking." One horse "constantly reared and caused disorder throughout."

Resting at the School for five days, Caron watched two parades by the cadre in the *manège*. The *écuyers'* parades do not appear to have given him enthusiasm, but he was dazzled by those of the jumpers at liberty that beguiled him as "incredible."

He assiduously followed the work of the *Sous-Maîtres* and declared himself "filled with wonder" this time by the results that they obtained in their dressage using the new method under the direction of the *Écuyer en Chef*.

Invited to the Cadre's *Sous-Officiers* mess, he was struck by their bad disposition in regard to the *Écuyer en Chef*, and at their scoffing at the training that they executed under his orders.

He noted furthermore that at the School, everybody had blood on his spurs. However, in Paris, at M. Baucher's lessons, no one had seen a drop.

Having returned to Paris, Caron struck up a friendship with Rul. Thanks to Rul, he obtained free entry to the Cirque des Champs-Élysés (it cost 0 fr. .50 for the military). He attended all of Baucher's presentations, unfortunately rare at that time because of his frequent absences. He made acquaintances, again thanks to Rul, of the personnel at the circus and was presented to Franconi, Paul and Pauline Cuzent, etc.

CARON, MASTER OF MANÈGE

In 1843, Caron was discharged "with a semester of leave" until his release, and he returned to Lille. In Douai, 1844 – 1845, he bought the material sold at auction by the Horse Post that had been disbanded following the development of the railway. He set up a business renting carriages and gave some lessons in an enclosure open to the sky. In 1846 or 47, the enclosure was covered, and Caron prepared to transform his establishment into the "*École de Dressage et d'équitation*" that lasted until 1914. In 1847- 48, he followed two new courses with Baucher, one with group lessons directed at "student teachers of equitation" and the other, private, for *Haute École*.

He found important modifications in Baucher's teaching:

The use of the whip on the chest to make the horse walk forward, before and during the flexions; the considerable importance attributed by the Master to the relaxation of the jaw that had replaced seeking the *ramener* as the principal and permanent preoccupation; the reduction by half of the amplitude of the lateral flexions where the horse only had to face to the right or to the left but not to the rear; the considerable decrease in frequency and duration of the rein back. For the *Haute École rassembler*, he noted that "the fury of the spur" provoked the twisting of the tail and that the mares "watered the *manège.*"

In 1849, Caron opened his *manège*. Twelve to fifteen horses hardly sufficed for his clientele that included notably the *Garde Nationale* mounted squadron, in which the entire well-off bourgeoisie wanted to take part.

Until 1855, Caron profited from Baucher's short sojourns in Paris between tours outside of France to come to the Capital "in remount." Baucher showed him a great deal of friendship, signaled to him to buy horse and sold him those that he had trained but that he wanted to be relieved of, whether because of their lack of capability or because of defects that did not allow them to be presented in public. It was in this way that a horse called César, having become a roarer after an inflammation of the chest contracted at the end of his training, was for a long time the pride of the *Manège de Douai*. "Baucher did not like to sell the horses that he got rid of in Paris, and preferred to see them leave for new homes as far away as possible, deep in the provinces." Rul, who had taken over the *manège* in Reims, profited from the situation just as Caron did.

In 1856, Caron noted that Baucher "was having difficulty recovering from his accident" and "that he is quite diminished." Caron's trips to Paris were less frequent because he had found in Belgium a better deal on the horses that he needed. It does not seem that he received special lessons on the "Second Manner" directly from Baucher, but he discussed it with Rul, who had not been successful in Reims and did tours in France and abroad to teach the new procedures. Rul overflowed with enthusiasm as always. Caron appeared less seduced, and does not seem to have altered his practices.

Until 1870, the business at the *Manège de Douai* was very prosperous. The North had gotten rich with the development of sugar refineries. Halted by the war, in which Faidherbe's Army requisitioned all of Caron's horses, the business was re-established afterward.

Caron saw Baucher again for the last time in 1872, a year before his death. "He is nearly blind; and does not leave his armchair at all." Without being in financial trouble, Baucher had been obliged to "count" since the pension that the Emperor had given him had defaulted.

Around 1850, Caron had brought to Baucher one of his cousins, younger than him by about ten years, named François Caron. The young man had worked at the *Manège de Douai* and showed a great disposition for the work of the School. Baucher engaged him to manage his stable during his trips, in which François Caron followed him for five years to all the great cities of Europe helping the Master in his training, and little by little, Baucher initiated him into all the finesse of spectacular equitation. Later, François Caron set himself up in Saint-Petersburg where he received the title of *Écuyer du Tsar*, which comported the management of the Imperial *Manège* and serious financial advantages. He was *Maître* to Fillis who dedicated to Caron his work "*Principes de Dressage et d'Équitation*" (See James Fillis, *Princliples of Dressage and Equitation*, Xenophon Press, Franktown VA, 2005) and who became in his turn, in 1898, *Écuyer en Chef* at the Cavalry School at Saint-Petersburg until 1910.

APPENDIX II – LOUIS SEEGER'S PAMPHLET

Over half of the copious brochure by Louis Seeger is devoted to the explanation of his own method.

After sharply reproaching Baucher for presenting his own method as superior to all others, Seeger made the same mistake.

Since the explanation of Seeger's method is without interest for the reader, Seeger's method will be mentioned only in the parts of the text that address the two methods at the same time.

(Author's Note)

EXCERPTS FROM:
"MR. BAUCHER AND HIS ART: SERIOUS WARNING TO THE RIDERS OF GERMANY"

By Louis Seeger

Pamphlet published in 1853 in Berlin against the propagation of the Baucher Method

Translated from German to French by Commandant Dupont,

Translated from French by Michael L. M. Fletcher

MONSIEUR BAUCHER AND HIS TOURS DE FORCE

"I do not want a system that detracts from the impulsion of the horse."

Duc de NEMOURS

We have recently procured the opportunity to closely examine the method of *"Maître,"* M. Baucher by seeing his personal practice using his own method. He has, by his

"New Method of Equitation," made an extraordinary impression during his lifetime. M. Baucher has audaciously thrown down the gauntlet at all other methods by presenting his own method as the only one supportable, as the only salvation of equestrian art that now lies in ruins. Up to now we have been able to judge M. Baucher theoretically.

Because I have constantly been declared the adversary of his method, as much in my *System der Reitkunst* (*System of the Art of Riding*, Xenophon Press 2011) as in my other books, one could expect from me a categorical declaration in this quarrel, which is pursued in various countries with diverse arguments, but has yet to be resolved.

It is also from duty that I consider myself obligated to make this declaration, because I hope to prevent grave damage. Since I am more specially qualified than many others to judge and because Monsieur Baucher, in whom I recognize great amiability, very much wanted me to ride horses that he had trained according to his method. I have ridden them as he indicated I should. He very much wanted to express his satisfaction to me, and I believe myself qualified to think that I finally succeeded in putting the horses into correct balance – following this *Écuyer's* personal concept. I have also frequently had the occasion to see Monsieur Baucher work horses in the process of being trained and so I am able to make a complete assessment.

I think that the sensation produced in the public by M. Baucher's method results from this *Écuyer's* talent for presenting his horses while conjuring tricks likely to impress the crowd. One could keep quiet about how widespread this impression is in France after an already long practice of M. Baucher's new method as well as the results that it has obtained to date. One could do that all the more because, after the demonstration of results that came to be made before our eyes, it is pertinent only to decide if this method presents something appreciable, acceptable to us, as Germans, in view of the equestrian goals that we are pursuing in Germany.

M. Baucher's method seems remarkable in that it constitutes a complete and closed system; a sequence so narrowly articulated that none of its parts can be eliminated without negating the value of the whole system. All of the elements are so intimately unified that one has to admit or reject the method outright – without anything being halfway envisioned.

It is from this single point of view that M. Baucher's method presents something original, because there is nearly nothing new in its particulars. M. Baucher is in effect less an innovator than an "adjuster" of various defective procedures put into practice for the corruption of equestrian art and the confusion of the students of the Duke of Newcastle and all the students of the Old Italian School.

M. Baucher has simply erected their errors into principles. He has been willing to present to a great number of bad trainers, even though perhaps involuntarily, they act as a mirror where their flaws can be perceived. Nothing therefore could be more advantageous for the world of riders than to have before their eyes M. Baucher himself in the application of his method – as an example of what they should avoid.

So, Baucher's method is not original. The only novelty that we might credit to this *Écuyer* is to have raised it to the level of a principle, and to have erected into a system, the *impairment of the natural impulsion of the horse* that has already crept into various bad methods.

We do not wish to directly reproach M. Baucher for presenting his horses *only* at the circus in Berlin. But, favorable occasions have doubtlessly contributed to the debate.

But this fortuitous circumstance is important because it most vividly brings to the eye the tight relationship that exists between M. Baucher's method and the goals pursued by the promoters of equestrian shows (circuses).

Since the Directors of the Circus have understood that the presentation of horses that are purely 'mechanized', or at least incompletely trained, fill their circus and their bank accounts at the same time, they naturally look to acquire the recipes for mechanization, or to have their horses mechanized by others, or even to exaggerate the mechanization themselves with their horses.

When the work of these horses is presented to the public as *"Haute École"* the directors gladly pardon this exaggeration by the *"Écuyers"* in two ways. Firstly by their ignorance, they present performances consisting of mechanical executions, devoid of higher equitation and of all the requisite preparatory training to higher execution. Secondly, they are obliged to address themselves to the purses of the ignorant people that form the majority of the public.

Connoisseurs of equitation should not expect to see perfectly trained horses, or school horses, at the circus because the small size of the ring, its circular shape, and the absence of corners permit neither correct dressage nor perfect execution. If any *écuyer* other than M. Baucher had made claims of *Haute École* at the circus, no one would have breathed a word because they would not have expected anything great.

But M. Baucher has posed himself as founder and prophet of an entirely new method that must be the one and only. He is the author of numerous works that have made him the talk of the whole world. This demands that we make a serious examination of his work.

It is inadmissible that a man as extraordinary as M. Baucher has exposed his reputation to the light in attempting to throw powder into the eyes of the German public by pretentions that he knows to be imperfect.

In these presentations that have been given in Berlin, we could see that M. Baucher presented the complete expression of his mastery. Given this proposition, the judgment that these presentations merited is also what the new method merits. Therefore we are going to first describe the presentations that we have been able to see each day at the Cirque Dejean, to first present the impression that results from them before making a tighter critical examination of the method, which will be appropriate later.

In the first place, M. Baucher merits as a writer a compliment that is not made to please him as an *écuyer*. From his books, of which the original form is full of grace and spirit, one gets a completely different idea of the rider. If M. Baucher would ride with the same ease, the same lightness that he shows in his amiable descriptions by presenting the paradoxes to, or insinuating himself into, the mind of the reader, he would have had an easier time introducing his system.

But anyone who possesses the least aptitude for observation is struck by the impression of constraint that is shown in the attitude of his appearance on a horse. His legs, perpetually stuck to the flanks of the horse and the stiffness of his torso give the impression of torment singularly far from the noble bearing, the assured ease, of the *Écuyers* of the good Old School. We must not give too much importance to this first impression since we should examine the new method only from the point of view of the effectiveness of its means to its goal.

I already have the sentiment that M. Baucher's manner must detract from his horses' impulsion: all those that he presented to us proved the truth in this opinion beyond all doubt.

M. Baucher's horses are not in their reins (on the hand), because they do not have the respect for the leg that is essential. Most of them manifest this lacking by wringing their tails. The hindquarters are totally outside of the position that allows the hind legs to have spring in their movements.

The lowering of the forehand takes away all liberty of the shoulders and eliminates all the energy in the elevation of the forelegs and all definition in the gaits.

These faults are manifested in all the gaits and airs that M. Baucher presents.

At the walk and trot, the forehand moves flaccidly and falls on the shoulders such that the hindquarters trail behind instead of pushing vigorously. The joints remain without elasticity because their "springs" do not come into play in their work.

The labored action in the trot partially escapes the spectator because M. Baucher's position gives his seat certain fixity and the perception of it is lessened for the rider by the fact that M. Baucher generally works, although for other reasons, on floating reins.

One rarely sees him take the tension on the reins that permits contact and then, only intermittently. One sees him on the other hand intervene frequently with his right hand on the curb reins to "pianoter[65]," according to his expression, and doubtlessly to supplement the insufficient tension on the snaffle reins, because without supporting contact, the bridle hand alone remains insufficient.

It is with reason that M. Baucher sharply cuts short his work at the trot, first because it displays the faults in his system too obviously and secondly because his work at the canter permits him to fool the public more easily.

We serious riders, who attribute more importance to the artistic value of the work than to its spectacle, have a principle that considers the trot to be the most important of all gaits.

For us, the trot is the base of all the others. The perfection or the ruination of the other gaits depends on the correctness of the trot.

In competitions, it is a characteristic rule that preference be given to the rider whose work at the trot presents all desirable polish even if his canter, on the other hand, leaves something to be desired, more than to the rider whose work presents the reverse characteristics.

According to this principle, M. Baucher's canter can only be defective – and indeed it is. Because his horses trail behind at the trot, instead of pushing, they hop at the canter, instead of bounding. This comes from the fact that M. Baucher completely neglects the flexion of the stifle joint which permits the development of elasticity of the hocks.

This is also the reason that M. Baucher does not "lift" his horses at the canter, but instead they "fall" in the canter and therefore canter on their shoulders.

In his work, the croup stays constant at the same level because the hind legs cannot engage due to insufficient flexion of the stifle joint.

---

[65] Play the piano; strum

Yet this engagement (of the haunches) is essential for the *rassembler*. The *rassembler* is also necessary for the preparation of the canter and the achievement of lightness.

M. Baucher's horses are not in *rassembler*, during the airs that he presents. His horses carry the dual mark of lack of impulsion and of acrobatics.

M. Baucher also executes his "changes of direction" completely differently from how we make our "turns."

These changes of direction are not correct pirouettes nor are they regular turns either because M. Baucher executes them with a predominant outside rein and outside leg so that it results in more of an irregular "curve."

Although for us, the horse, prepared by the inside leg and inside rein, enters progressively into his bend beginning with the forehand; M. Baucher's horse checks himself at first and then throws his body to the side.

It is up to riders to judge which is the better way of doing it.

For the changes of lead, M. Baucher impresses the layman by the execution of changes "at every stride."

As for us, we cannot do changes at every stride and we quite willingly leave this *tour de force* to him.

For us, the canter is essentially a "bounding" gait, and the change of lead requires a half-halt to collect, before beginning the canter on the new lead.

For M. Baucher the canter strangely approaches a "stepping" gait, the change of lead can be obtained suddenly; it is an exercise that can appear stunning for some people. The flying changes of lead every stride contribute powerfully to making the gait even more defective than it was before.

Perhaps I could please M. Baucher by properly explaining to him that his new discovery is doubtlessly nothing more than an amble but, under a new form, that of a 'canter amble.'

We wish him luck with this air for the sake of the preservation of his horses.

M. Baucher's *"parades[66]"* go together with his other practices that could not be better calculated to really ruin horses if one were to set out to do so.

They are made on the articulation of the haunches without the flexion of the stifle and with the fetlocks stiff. Since the hind legs are consequently incapable of adequate engagement, the haunches are insufficiently loaded. They continue to push the mass of the body with too much force and to overload the forehand.

In the rein back, M. Baucher's horses are in the same defective position.

Instead of being able to carry themselves behind as our horses do by the flexion of the haunches, they push themselves to the rear with their overloaded forelegs, and with stiff fetlocks. They do not march, they crawl. Since their hindquarters have too much freedom, they also have a great propensity to gain ground to the rear, and it is no surprise that M. Baucher does the rein back at quite an accelerated rate in a kind of trot.

In addition, it is the shoulders that furnish the greatest effort. This work presents an even graver defect. Crushed by the push of the stifle joint, the hind fetlocks stiffen and the fatigue in their joints is striking in M. Baucher's horses, as well as the weakening of their propulsive force. The push of the articulation of the haunch onto that of the fetlock, which is already naturally powerful, becomes particularly strained. When the push acts directly on the stifle, without being attenuated by the flexion of the patella, then the push power and 'springing' is lost.

Only the flexibility of the stifle allows the avoidance of fatigue in all the other joints, whatever the energy deployed.

Since M. Baucher does not obtain flexibility in the stifle of his horses, the use of the potential power of projection (springiness) that could be developed in the haunches, is totally unknown to this *Écuyer*.

M. Baucher has not executed the School jumps himself; instead we have seen them executed by horses that he has trained.

---

[66] Halts

These jumps consist of the elevating of the forehand started on a sort of bascule movement and terminated by the return to the ground of the forelegs before the hind legs. M. Baucher's horses do not know how to jump with suspension so that the four feet fall back to the ground at the same moment.

Perhaps it is more than co-incidence that M. Baucher's horses execute their jumps, not mounted by him, but by a woman. One is generally more indulgent of women riders than of *Écuyers*.

M. Baucher presents little work in the trot. The trot is the weakest part of his presentation, and before moving to a critique of his school work, it is necessary to observe that the gait that serves as a base for all the gaits in *Haute École* is the "school trot" which does not exist in M. Baucher's work. His horses are not up in front nor are they sufficiently on the hand.

It is precisely for this reason that we consider M. Baucher's method to be dangerous. The novice too easily confuses a school air with its pale caricature. They are amazed that such a result could be obtained in so little time.

Yet this result is nothing but a gross illusion.

The more M. Baucher showed his horse Blacknick, in Berlin, the worse the work became.

It seems that everything is backwards with this *Écuyer*. For us, each new reprise should bring progress in the work of our horses. The gaits should be reinforced and lightened at each session.

In the correct piaffe, we require that the horse keep the position of his body without altering it and we require that his legs move vertically in such a fashion that his feet fall back into the same place that they left.

M. Baucher's piaffe is quite different.

The legs are displaced laterally, because the stifle joint is not sufficiently flexed. The feet do not fall back into the same place that they left and the horse is required to balance himself in such a way that the distance between their tracks is greater than the distance from the shoulders to the haunches.

When the horse lifts his legs without pushing them forward, it is natural that the lack of flexion would force him to displace them laterally and lead to posing them in a defective position.

The hind legs in particular are insufficiently engaged and escape laterally or to the rear, despite the will of the rider.

It is because of this that in the piaffe, M. Baucher is obliged to use his aids so visibly with the brief attacks of the legs and spurs, by cuts of the whip on the hindquarters, by tugs on the mouth executed by seizing one rein or the other, etc.

The result is that the horse executes a shuttling movement back and forth without the forearms being sufficiently free from the shoulders. But the hind legs lift too high compared to the forelegs, and agitate like chicken feet.

In piaffe, as in all the airs, M. Baucher's horses lack the energetic movement and vivacity that the old French *Écuyers* called, "*tride*[67]." The German language does not have a corresponding word, although, thank God, *tride* has not ceased to exist in Germany.

This *tride* is also lacking in the passage of M. Baucher's horses because they lack energy and, as in all movements, are behind the hand.

Instead of offering the delicate pressure on the hand that comes with passage, the horses refuse it totally and are insufficiently collected for acquiring the powerful elasticity that gives the passage its impetus and suspension.

Thus M. Baucher is reduced, after having assured his seat, and intervened without discretion with his hands, legs, and his whip, to being on the forehand.

But in the true passage, the play of the aids must be invisible, and since reactions are null at this gait, the delicacy of the contact and fixity of the hand are very specifically facilitated (favored).

The least indication on the reins is sufficient to produce the necessary displacement of weight from front to rear and the

---

67   Lively, quick, short and united

increase in the flexion of the haunches that is enough to result in the determination of the gait.

For the same reasons, M. Baucher cannot obtain the School canter.

The canter consists of a series of bounds. These bounds are all the more elastic, all the more suspended and better regulated the better the weight of the forehand is transferred onto the hocks and consequently the bounds take advantage of the power of the spring in the hocks.

In the School canter, the position of the horse's body must remain constant.

The horse's body must make almost no movement and the horse's advance must be the result of only the movement of his hind legs that step under the haunches to lift again after being posed on the ground.

Generally, M. Baucher claims that the rider must only give the "position" to the horse, who must then by himself take up the corresponding gait – and we are entirely in accord with him on that, as it concerns the collected gaits.

But M. Baucher sins gravely against his own principles in his school canter. At first he shifts the weight for an instant to the rear and then leaves it to fall back on the forehand.

This visible ebb and flow of the centre of gravity, and the bascule movement that results, makes a painful impression on the connoisseur.

In summary, to differentiate clearly M. Baucher's canter from the Old School canter, one could say that our horse's body remains constantly parallel to the ground, while M. Baucher's horse's body is animated in a movement analogous to the motion of waves.

In the airs that M. Baucher presents as "canter on two tracks" and "terre-à-terre on the circle," his horses are thrown to the side while hopping, and if they use the inside hind as a support, they do not weight it sufficiently. Consequently they cannot receive the necessary impulsion from the inside hind leg nor use it as a pivot.

This comes principally from M. Baucher putting too much of his own weight on the outside hind.

It is also the same case with all the changes of direction, although M. Baucher excels in covering up this fault in the horse that is called "being behind the leg."

It results in the inside hind being pushed to the side by the outside hind and the haunches preceding the shoulders.

Outside of the fact that this canter on two tracks is very hard for M. Baucher's horses, again it lacks the particular precision in the placement of the legs, so characteristic of the terre-à-terre.

The *Redopp* is the terre-à-terre on two tracks on a volte, and the rocking that we described above in M. Baucher's canter strikes the eye even more here.

To be able to execute a measured and precise *Redopp*, M. Baucher's horses would have to begin their turn with the shoulders.

This turn must always be prepared by the action of the inside rein and inside leg, something that M. Baucher rejects on principle.

The haunches-out at the canter and the *counter-redopp* are yet more defective.

In this work, M. Baucher leaves all the weight on the shoulders and not in the middle of the horse. The hindquarters are too disengaged. Not only do they cover too much terrain but the hind legs deviate too much from each other.

To this list, add the pirouette. It is the last word in turns, one of the most difficult airs. The horse must change direction pivoting on the inside hind.

It is proof of arrogance to present a pirouette without certainly having done all the preparation necessary to the execution of this air, in particular the shoulder-in that has no other goal than to flex the inside hind, principally the stifle joint.

When the pirouette is achieved in all its perfection, the elastic power of the hock then permits the horse to lift himself on his inside hind, in such a fashion that this leg moves in place, and serves as the pivot point of the movement.

Only the elasticity of the hock allows achievement of a correct pirouette without the other joints being painfully overloaded, without the horse escaping the constraints of the movement.

What M. Baucher presents as a pirouette, it is a sort of stampede without flexion of the haunches. This ruins the fetlocks due to incomplete preparation and strengthening of the haunches.

M. Baucher does not pretend at all to use academic equitation, and we do not expect him to discover it in the rest of his work.

M. Baucher seems to have little taste – and probably with reason – for the airs above the ground in which the Old Masters placed all their pride. However, he has the fantasy to present the Pesade, which constitutes the route to those airs.

It seems that there again his horses' preparation is insufficient.

Instead of tucking the forelegs, as this air requires, in such a way that the feet nearly touch the elbows. M. Baucher's horses have a tendency to extend them as if to balance the overload imposed on the haunches. There is no proof more convincing of the insufficiency of the flexion of the haunches. Furthermore, by leaning forward during the pesade, M. Baucher shows that he does not have enough confidence in the strength of his horses' haunches to confer on them, in addition to the weight of the forehand, the weight of his own body.

That is also the reason that his horses stay in the pesade for such a short time and fall back to the ground so rapidly.

In summary, it is an faulty lifting of the forehand and not at all a pesade.

We have seen M. Baucher's horses – truthfully not ridden by him – execute jumps, but they were not School jumps. Furthermore, M. Baucher does not seek to execute that sort of jump, and it is natural that he does not present any academic airs above the ground.

I believe that I have sufficiently described in the foregoing all the presented work of M. Baucher that is remarkable and defective, and I have made it sufficiently intelligible to followers of equitation.

Before showing that M. Baucher's method must inevitably lead to defective results, I believe it necessary to describe exactly the tack and equipment that he uses.

The mouthpiece of his bit is always one piece, that is, without articulation[68]. It affords little freedom for the tongue with a shallow curve. The branches are straight and the attachments of the rein rings are fixed. The branches have rings to where is attached the lip strap.

Like M. Baucher, we hold this mouthpiece to be mild, that is to say of little effect, and we also use it with horses that are not completely trained when they still refuse to accept a firm contact. For complete training, in the majority of cases, we use for some time a bit in which the lever effect is more powerful, and we finish the training with a mild mouthpiece.

M. Baucher's bridoon has a ring of uncommon dimension. The headstall and the reins are of the English model, without a cavesson, and the curb reins do not have a button.

M. Baucher can do without the cavesson because he never rides his horses on a constant and firm contact and the horses consequently have no occasion to attempt to avoid the action of the bit by refusing the contact on the lower jaw, which the use of the cavesson has the goal of impeding. It is also for this reason and to enable him to "pianoter" that M. Baucher has removed the *bouton* from his curb reins.

M. Baucher uses his curb from the beginning of training, even with the horses that are newest to dressage. For the flexions of the jaw, from the beginning to the last stage of training, the action of the curb reins conforms to the goal that he intends more closely than does the action of the bridoon reins. M. Baucher uses them (the bridoon reins), nevertheless as I have already said, concur-

---

68   Joint

rently with the first (the curb reins) for the flexion of the jaw, of the head, and of the neck, from high to low and laterally.

M. Baucher's saddle has mainly the form of an English saddle but it differs essentially in its structure in the sense that it facilitates the position on the crotch that M. Baucher considers the only suitable one and that he maintains constantly.

This saddle makes the seated position, and our normal position, difficult.

The saddle tree is not made of wood but of very thick leather. The pommel is very pronounced. The points and bands of the tree are made of whalebone, held between two strong slabs of leather, on which rest the strips of steel that form the spring. The girth that passes over the twist of the saddle and serves to keep the saddle in place is fixed on the bands of steel that make the bands of the tree. (Teurkauff saddle)

When one girths the horse, these bands of steel bend in a way that the pommel and the cantle both the rise.

The seat is very soft and the cantle is more flat than curved.

The flaps are made of doubly supple leather and yield to the least pressure. The length of the forward part of the flap has a leading edge under which the padding is of an uncommon volume. The whole saddle is covered in rough and unfinished leather.

Finally the padding of the seat, which is very thick, is made of boiled horsehair.

Thanks to this arrangement, M. Baucher's saddle is extraordinarily elastic. Once girthed, the pommel and the cantle rise in a way that one finds it a little like a Hungarian military saddle (Bock).

Also it is perfectly favorable to the conservation of position on the fork so as to maintain a tight and permanent contact of the legs and knees with the body of the horse. It also continually throws the rider's weight onto the forehand, which M. Baucher considers to be the rule in his whole manner of riding.

The height of the seat and the cantle throws the rider's hips forward, and collapses the rider onto the crotch; this as a result of the girthing favors the verticality of the legs along with the position of the thighs and the knees flat against the saddle, the position necessary to the fixity and solidity of these parts of the body. The arrangement of the knee rolls and the adhesiveness of the leather covering contribute quite considerably to the position.

In our opinion, the position 'on the fork' is only appropriate in certain cases. It is only a temporary means and should not be used as a general rule.

We use it at the beginning of the training of young horses to set the weight of our body on the horse's shoulders and thus develop the aptitude of the shoulders to carry weight. We return progressively to the normal position, or to the seated position, and by this means develop the strength of the back and the hindquarters.

The application of these different riding positions should not just be statically applied for an entire lesson given to the horse, instead, during the different parts of the same lesson they can be utilized. M. Baucher's saddle does not allow using this technique and our saddle, when well constructed, therefore merits preference.

M. Baucher's spurs have a straight shaft and are very short. Their rowels are either completely round or are fitted with points that are greatly blunted.

To train a horse in the manner of the *"Maître"* (sic) Baucher, that is to say without developing his natural impulsion or even at the expense of it, particularly to obtain changes of lead at each stride of the canter, the incessant action of the legs and spurs with the continual clamping of the lower aids is required and results in a horse on the shoulders.

Formerly, M. Baucher used sharp spurs. Their perpetual stinging used to provoke the horse much more vividly and produced very noticeable twisting of the tail in all of his presentations as well as in his training sessions. M. Baucher now uses inoffensive spurs.

In the past, we hardly used anything but spurs with gooseneck shafts, fitted with sharp points set closer to the rider's heel than to the heel of the boot.

That allowed using a leg that remained elongated, without loss of time, without bending the knee, and without the approach of the lower leg. We even used those spurs with horses that have already finished the period of dressage called the "*relèvement*[69]." That is what is shown by the engraved works of the old departed *écuyers*.

M. Baucher uses the same kind of straight spurs with short shafts and blunted rowels, fixed to the buttress of the boot, from the beginning to the end of his training.

As far as I am concerned, to perfect the training, I consider it necessary to use these two kinds of spurs concurrently along with those that are presently in use that have rowels with five points of medium length.

In the period of "putting the horse on the hand[70]," I use spurs with round rowels most of the time. In the "raising of the head and neck" stage, I most often use spurs with sharp points, without occupying myself with the level of sensitivity of the subject when he is healthy and sound. For the last stage (3rd) of dressage, I employ alternately round rowels and those with blunted points.

But when one has no other goal than to teach a horse some tricks, one could be very content with round rowels. One could also do it when one rides a horse only in the 3rd stage of dressage – for lack of understanding how there must be a preparation for this stage by the raising of the head and neck – or because one does not know how to do it right.

The whip appears to be an instrument that is very necessary to M. Baucher. One never sees him without it, nor sees him ride without using it frequently.

---

69   Recovery, restoring.
70   *Mise sur la main*

For horses already completely trained and then ridden, M. Baucher uses the whip as punishment, with an extraordinary severity.

The mildness of his spurs is sufficient to explain the disturbing necessity for such harshness. Indeed no one with spurs so inoffensive could obtain the sensitivity to the legs, in particular to the pressure of the knee and that of the foot on the stirrup that the Old School described and considered to be indispensable for the perfection of the riding of a horse.

As to the power to throw his horse into a spin as our celebrated Cavalry General Seidlitz taught it, one can only get there by exciting the sensitivity of the horse to the effect of each of the two legs separately.

Often, it happens that the sharpest spur does not suffice and that it is necessary to revert to the use of a whip that is much more powerful than that of M. Baucher's. In such a case, the best is a whip of which the action is so much more energetic that its use becomes superfluous, particularly in the *"relèvement*[71]*."*

Concerning the use of the reins and the legs, M. Baucher postulates as the only rule: the action of the legs must always precede that of the reins. Never, according to M. Baucher, should the actions of the hand precede that of the legs.

We make the action of the legs precede that of the hands, as does M. Baucher, only when we want the weight to shift to the front and have it carried more on the shoulders than on the haunches. When we want to divide the weight equally on the forehand and haunches, that is to say to put our horse in balance, we make ourselves act simultaneously with the hand and the legs. When our horse is sufficiently advanced in his training to support increased weight on the hindquarters, or when we want to maintain it in balance by the flexion of the haunches, we make the action of the hands momentarily precede the legs.

That M. Baucher's horses are not exercised in the two preliminary stages of dressage that demand the application of the two

---

71   Recovery phase.

rules laid out above is shown to us only too clearly when his horses are put into the third stage.

M. Baucher has boasted to the sky that his equitation is allegedly in balance, but his art is nonetheless limited to the first stage of dressage and his horses only work on their shoulders.

If he would content himself, in the work on the shoulders, with lengthened gaits, we would not have anything to say about it; but he also practices all the collected gaits in the same balance, and executes all the airs close to the ground in the same way. Never would the Old School permit such a transgression of the rules of nature and art.

All the observations that I am making on M. Baucher's presentations are nothing surprising when one considers the entirety of his method of dressage.

I have seen M. Baucher work with my own eyes. I have ridden his horses and I believe myself able to speculate and say that none of the characteristics of his work have escaped me.

Ultimately his whole method tends to raise the force of resistance in a horse by weakening his natural tendency to forward movement.

Now I am going to first analyze all his procedures of 3rd stage training and compare them, when the occasion presents itself, with that of the Old School and to the method that I employ.

After M. Baucher had me ride "Blacknick" – and I will come back to that – he showed me his preparatory work. He showed me how he proceeds to make the newest horse, as well as those most habituated to service under the saddle, walk towards him by means of little taps of the whip on the chest and on the shoulders, combined with a traction on the curb reins, when the horse seeks to escape by backing up from the flexions of the jaw or from the lateral flexions of the neck. He then showed me the different degrees of these flexions, first in hand, then from the saddle.

Only two or three of these "manipulations" were new to me because M. Baucher invented them after the publication of his "*Méthode d'équitation*"[72] to replace certain others that he had exhibited and described in his book. These manipulations are for that matter so insignificant that one could very well not use them when one simply has to train a horse according to the principles of his book. That has no importance, provided that one knows exactly the dose of force that M. Baucher wants to see used in the flexion in question and how to find the exact moment at which one must release the action of the bits.

I needed to be instructed on this by M. Baucher himself, and it was only afterward that my opinion of this part of his training was formed.

Someone who has learned, following the rules of the Old School, to practice the effects of the curb reins in particular to gather in the head and to flex the neck, will commit some errors if they start flexion in M. Baucher's manner. One cannot in effect discern from this Master's book what scale is used to measure the force necessary in the traction on the reins and to determine the moment when one must release them; therefore one makes his calculation in the usual manner.

We are shocked by this Baucher procedure, whereby he wants one to invite the horse to put himself behind the hand by traction on the reins, only to give him afterwards a kind of recompense by releasing them. In our opinion, this evasion behind the reins is the source of all the flaws that any rider, however inexperienced, can easily notice in M. Baucher's horses.

Our preliminary preparation for putting the horse on the hand, consists, as one knows, of this: at first the saddle and bridle, all the while flattering the horse and talking to him; secondly and most important, putting him on the longe line to make him confidant and sociable and to habituate him to come in front of the action of the cavesson and the snaffle bit by himself, to which moreover he is incited by the man who holds the whip, whether by means of ample menacing or by a light touch of the whip, however without hitting him. This preparation is finished when the horse begins to take a firm contact on the bit, with the

---

72   See Hilda Nelson, *François Baucher, The Man and His Method*, Xenophon Press 2013

head and neck raised a little, and when he allows himself to be ridden easily – an operation over the course of which one must also keep the head and neck more or less raised.

In truth, M. Baucher uses an analogous procedure since he puts a new horse that is still too undisciplined for his flexions on the longe with the cavesson for some time. It is only the mounted horse that is not put into movement; he is kept, as much as possible, in place and one goes on to bend him following the already known procedure.

The question arises now is: which is the better procedure for preparing a horse for the *mise en main*; ours or M. Baucher's? In this instance, one must not lose sight of the fact that the essential goal of this preparation is not only to make the horse confident and to make him obedient, but to keep him keen.

The first impression that we make on the horse is obviously the strongest and the most durable. If then *a priori*[73], as M. Baucher prescribes, we employ the whip – and again while on the forehand – instead of caressing him and talking to him, to invite him to approach us, he will finish, certainly, by obeying, pushed by the fear of these punishments, and by carrying himself forward but he will do so only *with repugnance* and with a heightened suspicion.

So, because of that, the primary preparation given to the horse by Baucher is a preparation that is against nature; in my opinion this is the primary cause – among all those that I expose hereafter – for the lack of forward movement that felt so disagreeable when I rode his horses, and that compels M. Baucher, in the training of his horses and even during their exhibitions, to use the aids for forward movement, legs, spurs, or whip, visibly and nearly without interruption.

Our rules for the preparation of the horse in view of the *mise en main* and also of the achievement of his later education, the *relèvement* and the final stage of dressage, does not rest on arbitrary ways of seeing things that are personal to us; but they are borrowed from the very mechanism of the horse's movement.

---

73 Not based on prior study or examination; non-analytic.

For going from the halt to the walk, the horse prepares his balance in carrying the weight of his body forward distributed on the four legs in a way that the legs take on an oblique position, inclined to the front, then he throws his head and neck to the rear on the side of the foreleg that he wants to load.

The other foreleg, then unloaded, is carried forward while the raised head is pushed forward and the hind leg on the corresponding diagonal, engaging under the body, lifts and makes the body move forward again.

At each stride of the walk, as at the trot, this mechanism repeats itself and it is the more striking as the horse is more energetic.

M. Baucher does not comply with this natural law of movement. From the fact that the mass of the head and neck is brought lower, the four legs receive a distinct inclination toward the front and the two legs of a diagonal then generally make a step. But afterward, the form of movement is not the result of the action of the forces which the hindquarters (which act only when the rising of the mass of the head and neck is produced) carry and push forward provoking the impulsive effect of the horse. On the contrary, it is only the effect of the predominance of the weight of the forehand which carries with it the mass of the rest of the body.

By this direction[74] against nature impressed upon the head and neck, M. Baucher determines the cause of the movement falling on the shoulders, a fall that is notable in the horses that he trains. The liberty of the movement of the horse's shoulders can be obtained only by the progressive lifting of the head and neck. Also when one puts a young horse on the longe, when tacking up, one must not have the side reins impede the movement of the head so that he is able to carry it, with a certain liberty, forward and to the right and to the left.

M. Baucher, logically following his principle, that is to suppress the instinctive forces in the horse that push him forward, therefore does not make the horse depart right away after being mounted but rather executes the flexions he had

---

74 (Low flexion)

done before in-hand and even more if the horse has the desire to move forward. Should this degenerate into violent bounds, he then gets off and begins the flexion over again.

What concerns me is a shocking procedure that wants to practice flexions of the forehand with a horse that has not been prepared by forward movement and the raising of the head and neck and who keeps his four legs on the ground. Even more concerning, would be if after one has carefully made him work on the longe and then one is mounted in the saddle, the horse should refuse to carry himself forward – which is otherwise rarely the case. Any experienced rider carefully avoids putting his horse behind the hand by premature flexions, or making it worse by getting off after the horse has refused to go. The cause is too obvious to say anything more about it.

The second stage of M. Baucher's preparation of the horse consists of supplings of the hindquarters that, still more than the flexions of the forehand, are certain to extinguish impulsion since they have the effect of bringing lateral movements that are against nature to the hind legs that are the principal agents of forward (progressive) movement. By means of one of his hind legs in effect, the horse throws the other leg to the side to which it was invited by the rider's leg and the lateral rein.

By these rotations of the hindquarters, M. Baucher also aims to paralyze the natural forces of this part of the horse, and simultaneously, by the rotations of his neck, such that the horse cannot use them directly against the rider.

As soon as, in the rotation with the horse held in the grip of hand and leg (in the course of which the horse's head is placed in the opposite direction of the movement of the croup), the horse obeys, however little, M. Baucher goes from this movement to a rotation with the counter placement of the head. The croup is then pushed in the same direction as the head is bent. Finally, the pirouette is undertaken during which, as we know, the forehand describes a circle around the hindquarters.

I willingly concede to M. Baucher that such a lateral movement of the hind legs paralyses their force to the same degree as the flexions extinguish the horse's moral force, in addition to the forces of the jaw muscles and the extensors of the neck. Because, when his hind legs move to the side or cross over each other, the horse is as little capable of defending himself against the rider with the hind legs as he is to defend himself with his head and neck when they are kept far to the side and down. That is why the impression that Baucher's preparatory exercises momentarily make on the horse's energy is completely different from what we provoke following our normal exercises (work on the longe at the same time that one caresses the horse and speaks to him softly) and I think that this difference is not very much in favor of M. Baucher's procedures.

Indeed we find that after M. Baucher's preparatory exercises, the horses come back to the stable demoralized having gone back into themselves, while the horse that one has prepared and judiciously worked on the longe and has ridden with precaution seems much more exhilarated and joyful.

Just as M. Baucher's "flexions" leave the horse behind the hand; his "suppling" exercises leave the horse stiff in the joints of the haunches.

We do not possess any other means than the engagement of the hind legs and the related carrying of the weight of the head and neck on said hind legs for the suppling of the hindquarters of the horse, and in order not to hurt the mechanism of the movement, we must not admit into this period any other movement of the hind legs than that which brings them forward under the mass of the body; that is moreover the movement most naturally indicated for collecting the weight of the head and neck.

After that, by way of a sufficient training, the shifting of this weight becomes possible from the rider's hand, and only then do we mobilize the hind legs in other directions; however, in the movements to the side, it is the rule to execute them in such a way that the hind leg comes to pose itself in front of the other, but not beyond it by overlapping it, nor to the side of it.

By premature exercises on two tracks, in the course of which the fore and hind legs move on different lines, but also notably by the lesson analogous to Baucher's "suppling exercises": "head inside, croup outside," such as our Military School of Cavalry has in the past believed required for rapid training, the horse is put behind the hand and comes, as they said in the old days, "on the wrong haunch." The rotation of the hindquarters around the forehand fixed on one spot is a sufficient cause (for putting the horse behind the hand), and I must avow to M. Baucher that a stiffness of the haunches as in Blacknick and Rufus, I have perhaps found before on young or spoiled horses, but never yet on those that someone has had me examine as being trained.

To these movements of rotation of the horse in place, Baucher also associates the exercises of rein back, and with reason he attaches to these exercises a great deal of importance in the suppling of the hindquarters, to the extent that he has need for it in the horse's training. He is above all attached to a precipitated rein back in a movement that resembles a trot, because that is M. Baucher's principal means for the so modest flexion of the stifles shown by his trained horses.

By continual and precipitated rein backs, one can indeed with any horse, even one not prepared by this movement, come to constrain him more rapidly than by a measured walk to bend him in the stifle joints, if he, as is the case in general, stiffens these joints at the beginning; because the forces necessary to this resistance deplete themselves more rapidly in such a case.

M. Baucher has not paid any attention to those forces that we use right away to give the horse a firm contact on the hand and an extended forward movement because his goal is completely the opposite of ours.

In truth, he begins the exercise of rein back very prudently; he contents himself at the beginning with a few slow strides, in the course of which he does not at all weigh on the hindquarters, not even by his position because he leans forward still more than he usually does. By this prudent attention to the hindquarters, he aims at a double goal: on one hand to care for his own security, because if a horse that is not prepared for the rein back is persistently incited by the aids, he might easily rear, even until he falls; on the other hand, he seeks to make the horse take on a taste for moving backward, in a such a fashion as to make it easier for him later to take away the forces of the hindquarters by continual and precipitated rein backs.

When I experimented with the rein back on M. Baucher's horse, Rufus, in shifting my centre of gravity backward, I wanted to load the hindquarters, which were very vigorous but stiff, M. Baucher criticized me and said about the horse in general and of the hindquarters in particular: that it was a great fault to surcharge the hindquarters, and to want by doing so, to employ the part of the horse that was the weakest! It seems therefore that M. Baucher does not know in the least what great force resides in this part of the horse, which part he is pleased to name the weakest; or more likely, he knows it and he seeks – instead of freeing up and making the forces that sleep there useful, which evidently requires more time and effort – to treat the horse in such a manner that the horse unlearns the use of the force that resides in his hindquarters.

The lesson that M. Baucher gave me on Rufus's back gave me the key to the enigma: I knew from then on how one had to ride Baucher's horses, but at the same time what one was entitled to expect.

In general, we only practice the rein back at the moment when the horse, without the particularly predominant aids that are normal for forward movement, pushes in this direction onto the bridoon reins each tightened in its turn. It is then that the moment has come to collect him by means of the rein-back, or better to exercise him by this movement in the flexion of his hindquarters. If one practices the rein back sooner, one loses the principal goal of the exercise, that is to release the propulsive force of the hindquarters, and that is why M. Baucher shows again, in this case as in all the others, the little importance that he attaches to the true development of the propulsive forces of the horse.

It is now necessary for us to talk about the stage of M. Baucher's preparatory exercises that corresponds in some measure to our putting the horse on the hand. Truth to tell, M. Baucher aims here at the same goal as we do, that is: to confirm the horse's shoulders in their carrying force: but in contrast the means that he uses in this instance are totally different from ours.

What matters to us the most is a good gait in the horse; we carefully avoid therefore anything that could take away from his keenness, and from the first step forward, it matters to us principally to use and to educate the propulsive force of the hindquarters, so that the horse puts his head vertical instead of crooked or horizontal, provided that under the action of the aids or the corrections by which we push him forward, he takes a firm contact on our hand, or as one says, "the fifth foot." Naturally for that we need a fixed position of the poll and the neck, as well as the least painful mouthpiece that can be a simple service bridoon in skillful hands.

None of that with M. Baucher. In all of his work, he shows that what interests him is not so much a good vigorous gait but a means of easily removing the spirit of resistance in the horse. But if this means rests on the weakening of the possibilities of practical resistance in which, without contradiction, the horse still seeks his master – only limited minds could be left mystified by a training that, instead of making the horse more vigorous and at the same time submissive to the rider, probably allows him to obtain the latter result, but at the expense of the natural forces, and therefore of the general utility and useful value of the horse.

What sufficiently characterizes M. Baucher's whole method is his formula following which the rider has as much more power over his horse as the horse has more feet on the ground; from there come his exercises for preparation of the horse by immediately making the flexions of the forehand in place; from there also comes the formula that is found in chapter 147 of his *"Méthode d'équitation"* (1843 edition): "the walk is the mother of all the gaits!" We who work the horse in movement, because movement is his destination, we call *the trot* the mother of all the gaits, the one in which the horse has the least number of feet on the ground: the one that, pushed to its greatest energy as in the school trot, offers moments when not a single leg is found to be on the ground.

We now have to see how M. Baucher proceeds with this mother of all gaits and what he takes from it. It is to the collected walk that he gives preference when the horse carries himself forward for the first time; then he soon begins tight turns at close intervals, and only quite a long time afterward, the trot, which he also wants collected.

It is easy to see what he is aiming for. It is solely to keep the horse in movement in the same collected form that the preceding flexions in place have brought about.

This way of doing things is precisely opposed to what we look for in the course of putting the horse on the hand, since in this period we try hard to extend the horse in all measure possible by lengthening the walk and trot and principally by the free extension of the trot.

Since, as it happens, the turns, especially the tight turns, can only hinder us, we avoid them as much as possible and we make the horse move on a straight line.

Our goal is effectively the trot as a means to continue to develop the horse's forces. If it happens however that from mistrust a new young horse balks and refuses to take up the trot, we are forced to ride him continually at a slow walk and at most at a *trot marché*; but then we have no intention of making this walk a preparation for the other gaits. We only use the walk as a means to take away from the horse the mistrust mentioned above.

In this point of view, we bump up against M. Baucher. Because, he is under an illusion if he thinks, that by the practice of the walk in this period, he will get to the correct gaits. He uses the walk much more for acting on the horse's intelligence, and the effect obtained is reinforced by the numerous turns. But the fact of acting at this moment on the horse's intelligence and seeking there, so to say, a goal in itself, not simply the means to act in a firm and vigorous fashion on the horse's body, leads to nothing more than realizing a certain precociousness in the horse, thanks to which he is soon found to be in a state to perform all sorts of nice tricky movements.

But after these tricks, should the essential purpose of the use of the horse be forgotten, it will be impossible to develop the qualities corresponding to this purpose. It is obvious even.

This becomes still much clearer, if one thinks, given M. Baucher's method of preparation mentioned above with flexions, turns, and rein backs, that these exercises, repeated twice a day, can not fail to produce in the horse a persistent moral impression of such power that he really comes to imagine that these sorts of movements, as well as the tours de force that they make possible, are the desired result and essential goal pursued by the rider.

In his *"Méthode d'équitation"* M. Baucher has written of his work on the spur in a special chapter and in a more detailed way than have the authors of treatises on equitation before him, even those whose writings, aside from the images of their horses, we recognize as masters of the art. But it is notable in the modern era that they have a fear of avowing with what persistent severity it is necessary to use the spur if one wants to obtain the results that we aim for with our work on the spur. The reasons for this fear can be diverse; they are: in part, the fear of appearing too tyrannical to people; in part, the fear of confirming in their errors beginning riders who so easily let themselves to go to the abuse of the spur; in part also – it could be – because these old masters want very much not to ruin, by a sincerely believed hard training, to which they owe such perfection, the amiable charm that for the reader of their writings is in the images of their trained horses and the descriptions of their work.

But such a mutism has become extremely dangerous for equitation because the result is a lack of energy in the trainers of horses and this lack has opened the door to all these alternative means that while avoiding forceful means could however lead to some semblance of success.

The difference between our work on the spur and that of M. Baucher is very important.

Our way aims at instilling in the horse a fear of the spur such that he has no more need to actually feel the action of it after he has completely learned to recognize it; a fear such that the pressure of the leg, the calf, and the knee on the horse and the pressure of the foot on the pad of the stirrup suffice to overcome the aversion that he has to the action of the bit before the stick of the spur that would follow. Does the layperson perhaps find our spurs with long points to be dangerous? Yet their action is such that later, the horse does not need to be bothered by it because the mere memory of the spur suffices for any correction that might subsequently become necessary.

It is completely otherwise with M. Baucher. Truth to tell, his spur is completely blunted. But he uses it continually and the horse, his head insufficiently vertical in M. Baucher's low flexion, is tortured with pokes of the spur and cuts of the whip to an extreme degree that borders on cruelty. To add to that at the same time the horse placed straight is pushed to the side where it happens often enough that one leg strikes the other. Furthermore M. Baucher has clearly given me to understand that he does not like very much anyone seeing him work his horses when they are not completely trained to the attacks and consequently they would still resist him. It could be that he sees his manner of practicing the attack in such a way that he would prefer not to show it; such little secrets are truly not appropriate for a master of equitation and M. Baucher, him, the far too malevolent denigrator of the methods of others.

From his work on the spur, M. Baucher does not obtain results of the sort that we do, but his unfortunate horse sees, all his life before him, a prospect of continued attacks that the Master himself cannot do without over the course of his exhibitions; because in his horses, the sensitivity to the legs, instead of being intensified as in our work on the spur, is blunted by his, and as soon as the necessity of propulsive aids are felt, M. Baucher is obliged to use the maximum pressure of the legs and the poking jolt of the spur. His horses do not respond to actions of a lesser intensity,.

The relatively short time in which M. Baucher attains the goal that he aims for by his attacks can be surprising in some ways. But when one recalls what we have already said above, know that Baucher's flexions of the head and neck momentarily blunt the horse's sensitivity in the same way as a twitch, even in otherwise nervous horses. If one adds to this that during the exercises of rotation, turns, changes of direction, and of rein back, the horse has already put up with the contact of the spur for short moments, one sees it is not more than one step to arrive at the attacks, which more energetically compel the horse to abandon his instinctive forces.

It is natural that a stronger and persistent *ramener*, to which corresponds, on the hindquarters, the work on the spur, annihilates sensitivity still more; and with this relationship, the effect of the attacks is disheartening to the intelligence of the horse. The pressure from the rush of blood to the brain during the *ramener outré*, which the horse feels very rapidly, consequently renders him insensitive to the pressure of the legs on his sides and of the spur on his flanks.

In his introduction to the part of his method that deals with the attacks, M. Baucher maintains that, by the *ramener*, the natural or instinctive forces are distributed through the whole body of the horse; but he considers that by the work with the attacks, he concentrates these forces in a common centre that is the rider's hand. And then, by means of the attack, the force of the hindquarters is put into action forward, and there it is 'captured or paralyzed' by the opposition of the hand. M. Baucher claims in an expressive fashion that the resistance of the reins balances against the force that comes from the hindquarters. From where it results that, by the complete exercise, one does not obtain any other centre of gravity than the one in which the vertical falls between the shoulder blades, as already was the case in the *ramener*.

M. Baucher asserts that he holds the concentrated forces of the horse in his hand, their common centre, he must however recognize that there exists at least one force that makes an opposition to those forces and that is weight, since the centre of gravity of the horse is not situated vertically under the hand but much more forward. But, even if the centre of gravity is found to be vertically under the hand, it would not be – and by far, given the inclined forward position that M. Baucher adopts – under the middle of the horse – as our author imprudently holds at the same time. Therefore his nice symbol that the forehand and the hindquarters of the horse are the arm of a scale and the rider is the arrow marking the break of balance is nothing other than a seductive phrase of which the inexactitude easily appears to any rider that reflects on it.

Generally, M. Baucher's explanations are of a weakness so striking that one would not finish if one would want to unveil all his errors, as well as the contradictions that nearly all in one breath he spreads in his Method. Thus he constantly negates in one clause the principle of which he makes a triumph in another. Attentive critics could not keep from thinking that always in the precise place where M. Baucher has placed a particularly striking sentence, it is only to mislead, because not only the question of truth, pure and simple, furthermore the declarations that he makes in other places bring out a contradiction too flagrant for it to be a simple inadvertence.

With M. Baucher's "*rassembler*," it is even worse than his "attacks." As in all of his exercises, he essentially distinguishes himself from the old school.

The old French Masters of equitation understood by "*rassembler*" an action thanks to which the horse, advancing his hind legs under the mass of the body by the gesture of a step or a bound, is rendered capable of making a more or less large part of the weight of his forehand shift to his hindquarters; in other words: by the *rassembler*, one positions the horse, placing his forehand by bending his hindquarters in such a way that the shoulders and the haunches will be called upon to support the weight of the body, either in an equal manner or with the predominance of the weight on the haunches.

From the very beginning, German riders had very precisely interpreted the sense of this important problem posed by the old school. Indeed they habitually spoke of a horse "*which collects*," consequently thinking less about the rider's activity than that of the horse; and that is exactly correct, since according to the principle in question, the rider must simply set up the horse and it is up to the horse to displace the weight.

However, since they think that they are able to reject the teaching of the old school, they hardly ever speak of bringing the horse to "se *rassembler;*" and one hears nearly nothing but the expression "to take in the hand and concentrate," which clearly indicates a greater activity on the rider's part while the horse in this case behaves rather passively.

M. Baucher has a habit, already inveterate, of neglecting the old school and its method of equitation: because when he came on the scene with his system, neither master nor students knew much about what was a correct *rassembler*; Baucher's theory, which has the greatest resemblance to that of "take in the hand and concentrate," falls therefore on fertile soil, and while he puts the greatest pride in having invented something new, precisely these novelties only find an echo because riders have executed something analogous for a long time. This theory was however like the Savior that they considered him to be, because in the general distress he brought a means of help and he boldly posed as cardinal virtues and as a principle the weaknesses that, perhaps in secret, one could well be ashamed of.

Naturally, when a method teaches that the horse must be brought to the most complete passivity and become absolutely a machine under the rider, the method is welcome to all those who lack the judgment and the energy necessary to dominate a living being and to arrange his instinctive forces without part of the forces being taken away from him.

But that a powerlessness of the horse so complete should call for a continual tutelage on the part of the rider so that the rider lose in liberty precisely what the horse loses in force is a point that laudatory admirers and imitators, way too impressed by Baucher, would certainly have to take into consideration before blindly throwing themselves into his arms.

After M. Baucher has made his horse, at the halt, walk, and trot, on one track and on two tracks, in the rein back, in the turns in place with the placer "*plié*" and the counter placer, and finally, in turns of the genre of pirouette, take on the habit of supporting his attacks without disturbing the low flexion of the head and neck, he moves on to his "*rassembler.*"

He chooses, for this effect, the moment when he has "prepared" the horse so that it is straight and has his four legs vertical. With his nearly rigid hand and his legs very tight, he now carefully checks the fixity of the horse's head and neck as well as the croup. By a very cleverly calculated action of the legs and the spurs which act first, he brings the horse to carry his hind legs forward up to the line of the haunches while his forelegs noticeably mobilize in place or advance very little and stay very close to the ground. In the beginning, a slight mobility of the hindquarters is sufficient for M. Baucher to decide to release his constraint, and only a few exercises are sufficient to habituate the horse to forward movement that is more a sliding or a stamping than a stride of walk.

When M. Baucher's horse is *rassemblé* to the extreme, one could say that the horse wants to shorten himself just as he would if he wanted to lie down; that way, he forms an almost circular figure from the end of his nose to his hind feet; and in these conditions, the more the curb reins are forcefully held, the more the lower jaw approaches the chest, or the neck, and the more the hind legs approach the middle of the body.

Then the effect of the reins does not go to the back of the head at the first vertebra of the neck, and to the second, but from the mouth directly to the third, often even to the fourth vertebra, following which the position of the head and neck is more or less low; the first two vertebrae are outside of constraint. That is the reason for which M. Baucher cannot make these two vertebrae yield, not more than just the poll by means of persistent traction of the reins. He is therefore required to have recourse to "piano-ing" on the reins, to turning, to changes of direction, to shortening of the lessons, even the length of time of work in the lesson, in sum to rapid successive changes in his various exercises.

The effect of Baucher's *"rassembler"* needs to be studied in more detail; because this study is of an extreme importance for understanding the effect of the application of his *rassembler* on the defective gaits in his horses.

To incite the horse to engage his hind legs, one employs the spur or the leg, of which the action, here as throughout the

Baucher procedure, precedes the action of the hands; afterwards there is a place for the traction on the reins.

But given the *"ramener"* position of the horse, this traction cannot act "as a lever," from vertebra to vertebra, from the first vertebra of the neck all the way up to the sacrum, and from there, against the hock; to the contrary, as the whole forehand forms a compact mass, so to say, on which one pulls, the effect of the traction propagates directly from the mouth to the hindquarters in a nearly horizontal direction.

As a result of the low position of the head, this horizontal line falls, under the stifle joint, directly onto the hock and by the intermediary of the hock, onto the fetlock joint; from where for the latter comes the predominant effort, which is a gross fault, since the articulation of the pastern, manifestly, is the weakest of the two.

How much is this harmful and dangerous for the conservation of the hindquarters: it is useless to demonstrate.

But the drawback consists not only in the fact that the articulation of the pastern is submitted to the predominate effort; from the point of view of the effect of this on the horse, there is still the much more important drawback that the impulsion can only be weakened by an effect of this kind against the hindquarters.

Impulsion rests in the whole hindquarters of the horse and can only be developed in an energetic manner if by an appropriate flexion of the upper joints, that is to say the haunches, and by an effect of opposition of the lower joints, that is to say the articulations of the pastern and the hoof, it is concentrated in the hock.

The flexion of the stifle joint pulls down the upper part of the femur; the pressure of opposition of the pastern in a sort of reaction from the ground, pushes up the lower extremity of the tibia; and thus is produced, in the hock, that energetic flexion that develops the full force of the spring particular to this articulation and permits the haunch to produce the movement forward whether in bounds or at a steady and measured walk.

Since M. Baucher, in the *rassembler*, does not bend the stifles sufficiently, the hock forms an angle too obtuse to be able to develop its force as a spring. Therefore in this position, any traction on the reins, instead of favoring impulsion, can only weaken it. What should I say? Even limply supported, it can only bring the horse's gait to become lifeless.

That is why M. Baucher is obliged – and he holds to it severely – to make a new release immediately after each traction on the reins, so as not to stop the movement forward. But, by this release, he obtains nothing other than this result: that again the mass of the forehand falls to the front dragging the hindquarters after it, instead of it being the hindquarters that give the impulsion and raise the forehand by pushing it.

This hindrance of impulsion, specially produced by Baucher's *rassembler*, is so striking that the horses entrusted to this *écuyer*, after having developed their liberty of the shoulders at the trot thanks to dressage by earlier trainers, essentially do not lose this liberty with him until the *rassembler* phase; but as soon as they are exercised at the *rassembler* according to his method, they very soon lose this quality. We have seen this fact verified here, in Berlin, at the Royal *Manège*, in a fashion most certain; because, of all the horses that by his order have been worked there under his direction according to his method, *not one of them conserved the free trot that he possessed naturally or that he had learned* before being allocated to M. Baucher. I have personally had the same experience with the horses that as a trial, some years ago, I have ridden according to the Baucher method, which made me from then on, an adversary of this method. Now that I have seen M. Baucher in person, in Berlin, I am convinced that no incomprehension on my part has skewed those previous experiments.

To anyone who knows the correct *rassembler*, the manner in which M. Baucher bends the haunches for the *rassembler* can only appear extremely blameworthy. Yet, this *écuyer* insists heavily on the fact that before him the *rassembler* (his, the one that he teaches) had never been exactly understood or explained. As it concerns this last point, we can agree with him, but in the old school, they understood his *rassembler* very clearly, but they were not inclined to teach it because, on the contrary, they presented it as constituting a grave fault. They were familiar with this wrong work well before M. Baucher was around, and they designated it with the expression, "To put the horse on the wrong haunches" (To put the horse falsely on the haunches).

The Duke of Newcastle, who be it said in passing already practiced a *ramener* analogous to that of M. Baucher, also put his horses falsely on the haunches, as one can see quite well in the copper engravings in his treatise on equitation as well as in the oil paintings that are found in one of his properties now belonging to the Duke of Portland – engravings and paintings that have faithful portraits of the Duke of Newcastle's horses.

If M. Baucher wants us to retort that the *true rassembler*, ours, the *rassembler* obtained by the predominate flexion of the stifle joint, has not been taught in the works in the celebrated schools of the old *écuyers*, notably de La Guérinière, he commits a gross error. Without a doubt, they have not, as has M. Baucher in his *"Méthode d'équitation,"* spoken of the *rassembler* as one might speak of the Good Lord and those mysteries that are inaccessible to the understanding of man; but, in a fashion very instructive to us, they have explained how, through the *rassembler*, one can obtain the flexion of the articulations of the haunches, notably the flexion of the stifle joint, and how, in short, the whole art of equitation rests on that flexion of the haunches. If their works also do not contain a chapter carrying the special title "The *Rassembler*" as does M. Baucher's method, these works give us however the conviction that their authors deeply understood the *rassembler* and knew how to make it understood. On the contrary, we would very much like to see from where in M. Baucher's chapter entitled "The *Rassembler*" one can draw an intelligible definition.

But what comes out of our exposé of his *"rassembler"* is that the famous concentration of forces that he thinks he has obtained by his attacks and by the *rassembler* is an illusion, that the hindquarters of his horse have constantly too much liberty, that, as a result, the forces of the hindquarters are not in his power, and that, consequently, he cannot make them usable.

In his *rassembler*, M. Baucher pays for not having practiced the raising of the head and the neck, our procedure from

"*Dressur.*" Any horse that has not been submitted to this exercise refuses to flex the stifle joint, without which one cannot *rassembler* in a manner where the horse conserves his keenness in full.

What advantages are possessed, on the other hand, by our *rassembler*, when the horse has been prepared appropriately by the raising of the head and neck, one can see, after all that has been said above, in a rather evident manner. However to be more complete, it is still necessary that we put our principles alongside those of M. Baucher, now that we have clarified these last points.

In our "Dressage Procedure," a new training period starts with this work on the *rassembler*. Whereas, indeed, until the achievement of the raising of the head and neck, our goal was to prepare to place the horse (in *ramener*, round, likely with a bend) while he is in forward movement, we now begin to seek, by that placer, a new sort, but a superior sort, of forward movement. By the procedure of the raising of the head and neck, the horse's way of going has been trained in a manner so complete that one can now be sure that one can no longer bring him harm if one demands of the horse a work that is no longer lengthened, but that, in other terms, is more *rassemblé*.

The placer that collects the horse in no way impedes the impulsion. But the impulsion no longer acts directly in a straight line toward the front with the force predominately carrying the shoulders. To the contrary, it is principally the haunches that are called upon to work, and that in an oblique direction sloping from the forehand to the rear. There the springs of the hocks are compressed and the impulsion now must take a direction opposed to that in which the hock has been compressed, thus from low behind to upward and forward. By such movement any shock and any kind of jolt is reduced or eliminated, great precision is established in the gait, and, at the same time, all parts of the horse are used more in line with their possibilities because of better balance that is less fatiguing to the horse.

We are now going to go into more detail.

In any appropriately prepared session from *"Dressur,"* there are moments when the rider, while he lifts the horse's head or even puts the horse in the *ramener*, can take a solid point of support, that is to say to energetically support the tension on the reins. Then if by means of the legs or the spurs, he makes the horse engage his hind legs under his body, in such a way that the hind legs, principally by the flexion of their stifle joints, take up the weight of the forehand supported on the reins, then they compensate by their coiled spring position for the part of the horse's weight that is thrown against them.

In this position, the horse is now in a state to distribute his and his rider's weight together from the hindquarters onto the four legs and to maintain himself in *rassembler* for a more or less large number of strides. Because in the alternative movements of posing and raising the hind legs, the hocks nearly without our intervention now develop their spring force for some time and when this force wanes, it is enough for us to place the horse so that he will collect again.

If the hind leg in movement does not come into the position of a spring, the horse cannot collect correctly. But how far is it necessary to push this position? To a degree more or less great according to how the rider has more or less brought the horse closer to placing the balance of the forehand and is able to keep it there, but to the degree at the same time that the horse obeys the rider's legs and spurs to lift and engage the hind legs, otherwise said – according to the current expression – to the degree that he possesses respect for the legs.

To bring a horse to an absolutely perfect *rassembler*, it is necessary before anything else to have obtained the ultimate degree of raising of the head and neck described in the explanation of the procedure in *"Dressur."* At this degree, the horse shows himself ready to bring his hind legs right away into a position of a compressed spring under the effect of the legs and spurs, thus to push his centre of gravity toward the midline, then on an effect produced almost only by the hand, that is to say on an equal and progressive action of the two reins, to push his hind legs still more forward, while he bends in the stifle joint, lowers his croup and brings his head close to the vertical with his neck lifted, curved like a swan neck, that is to say carrying the head in an oblique angle from the poll, but not vertical.

In this position, the horse's centre of gravity is backed up and lowered, the action of the reins, formerly rigidly tight, is almost only felt by their weight; and now it is left to the horse to act during forward movement with the shifting of the centre of gravity toward the middle of the body where the rider must then seek to keep it by the simultaneous action of the hand and leg so as to maintain the balanced position that has been obtained this way.

How much differently on the contrary does M. Baucher proceed to shift the centre of gravity in the course of his *rassembler*. Just as he cannot keep the centre of gravity to the rear, much less to the middle of his horse's body, he is only capable of carrying it from front to back momentarily, leaving out the midpoint; and that is a fact that obliges him to *pianoter* and to use his legs nearly incessantly, and from where comes the result that he is not in a state to act, to a greater or lesser degree, with the horse's head as a weight and his neck as a lever arm along with the position and movement necessary for our *rassembler*.

To this end we now act with the forehand against the hindquarters more often and for a longer time than before. Consequently we work the horse in third degree exercises, that is to say in high dressage, longer than in those of the first and second degree, in which we put him on the hand and raised his neck and head; we seek, by shortening the time of forward movement, to hold the too ardent impulsion of the haunches in the bridle, in the literal sense of the word, from which impulsion we instead develop more the force of the lift to be able, in the final accounting, to balance it with that of the shoulders.

It is only now that we use the curb bit that because of its lever effect is a tool more appropriate for the last stage of dressage than the stable snaffle.

We know that according to their intensity of action, one qualifies the curb bit as mild or severe. For the last stage of dressage, we first use mild bits, but later to confirm the horse, more severe bits. Because to be able to use the bit's complete effect of the lever, that is to say to be able, by means of the forehand to regulate the hindquarters, it is necessary that the horse be familiarized beforehand with this mouthpiece that is new to him. To this end, the bit the most indicated is the mild bit in the genre of that which M. Baucher himself uses; it is the least uncomfortable for the horse, since by virtue of its flat and shallow tongue passage, this bit acts more on the flat side parts than on the often very sharp edges of the bars, which besides are protected by the tongue like a cushion; and we know that the pressure on a fleshy part is less bothersome than on bone or a boney ridge.

The bit with the least lever effect has for us, in this period (precisely the inverse of M. Baucher) the advantage of paralyzing less the action of the bridoon when it acts to prevent the horse from burying his head to hold himself back and come behind the hand; therefore it permits us to confirm the horse in the correct *ramener* and to prepare him to *"se rassembler."*

When we have achieved this end, by means of a mild bit, and when we have worked the horse in the *pli*, or the placer for the trot, in the counter shoulder-in position, or the placer for canter in the position of shoulder-in, or the position of counter-canter, then when we have, with these different sorts of positions, alternated more or less tight turns and changes of direction at 3 gaits, and lastly when we have habituated the horse not to recoil from objects that make him afraid, we will consider him to be sufficiently trained for normal use by, for example, a rider of 2nd class or a private individual.

If we want to *rassembler* the horse and mobilize him in this unique goal, we have no need of a bit with a lever effect, or a severe bit; because on the one hand by our balanced position of the forehand, on the other hand by the flexion of the stifle joint, we have taken possession of the poll and from that, of the neck, and the horse has now acquired respect for the hand and the legs and a reflexive obedience to these aids, as well as the liberty of the shoulders that is necessary for ordinary service.

On one hand, by our placing of the head and neck, which are most importantly coming out *high*, on the other hand by the *rassembler* obtained as a result of the flexion of the stifle joints, we have a considerable advantage over the "concentration" that Baucher and other *écuyers* obtain by the position of those same parts coming out *low*. The advantage is that if we have horses that go with the head and neck too highly placed and who are against the reins by their nature or because they are resisting us, we have no need while correcting them to begin by lowering the head and neck and by that perhaps to shorten the horse's stride, but we can do it with the head in a higher position and without the loss of ground. Because the force of the extensors of the head and neck, with which, in this case, the horse is resisting us, is broken by the flexion of his stifle joints – flexion to which our horse, neck already raised, lends himself voluntarily, if we invite him, to "se *rassembler*." Furthermore an indirect correction of this sort acts in a much more lasting manner than any action directed against the extensors for flexing the neck and lowering the head.

What is more: against the opposite defense, that is to say when the horse puts his head and neck out of control, placed too low, and he plunges downward in his reins, there does not exist a means more simple and more correct than our *rassembler*, since by flexion of the stifle joints, the croup is lowered *vertically* and from that, the head and neck can be put back in place more easily. Moreover, the preparation for the *rassembler* by our procedure of raising the neck and head make the horse lose this defect exactly to the same degree as when, on the contrary, it becomes ingrained, if one puts the horse, who is inclined to that fault, falsely on the haunches by "concentration".

M. Baucher rejects the bit with a lever effect or a severe bit because he does not need it for his *ramener* and his *rassembler*; because in this case, he makes maximum use of the lever of the forehand, up to the middle of the horse's body, and not, like us, of the lever of the hindquarters.

Yet this latter action is absolutely necessary to put the horse into *ramener perfectly* and to be able to put him into the *rassembler* as his *complete* use demands.

The complete *ramener* requires in effect, as we have already mentioned, not only that the neck be raised and supported in a fashion generally sufficient for the normal use of saddle horses, but more yet that, by bringing the head in, the neck bends into a swan neck with the head, while not losing its oblique position in relation to the poll, coming to the vertical position. For this effect, the mild bit generally does not suffice for us and for some time then we use more or less severe bits according to how we propose to act in a fashion more or less depending on the corresponding placement of the two levers of the horse's body.

With this severe bit, we do not attach much importance to whether or not it has long branches as are used voluntarily by riders who put the horse into *ramener* by placing the head vertically; but what makes the value of the severe bit is its larger passage for the tongue, in a noose, as they say, that allows the hand to have its point of support directly on the lower jaw, and this always by virtue of the general principle that is necessary in the training for obtaining a perfect saddle horse to act in a predominate fashion on the firm parts of his body.

It is perhaps by the description of the maximum necessary effect of the (curb) bridle that our manner of positioning the horse for the complete *rassembler* is explained the best. The horse, having been perfectly prepared by the *relèvement*, one could imagine him under the rider in a state of rest, the head and neck raised, the hind legs engaged and ready to spring. If then, by an equal traction on the reins, the head is pressed against the two facet joints of the first vertebra of the neck, the horse begins by carrying the head and neck to the rear, then it bends the latter into a swan neck and gives us the flexion of the *ramener*. The traction, continuing its force, now acts in the same manner along the whole spinal column all the way to the sacrum and, from there, to the articulations of the haunches and the hocks, where in bending these parts, it achieves its goal.

That is the moment when the horse is perfectly placed for the *rassembler*. Now, under the effect of the weight of the forehand coming from up backwards, the hocks develop their spring force that makes the horse move from the state of rest to the more or less energetic state of movement according to the degree of *rassembler*, movement, over the course of which our legs, that beforehand put the horse into action, now have no more to do than to prevent the hind legs from leaving their position as springs.

By this perfect *rassembler* the rider becomes absolute master of the horse and all of his forces, and, all parts of the animal's body being in harmony, he can obtain by means of relatively light aids the most remarkable results, with which those of M. Baucher can not in any way stand comparison.

By the remarks that we have made on the subject of Baucher's *rassembler*, we have sufficiently demonstrated that this *rassembler* does not permit in any way the rider's concentration of the horse's forces to a degree such that he would not be required to continually intervene in the hindquarters. What therefore is more natural than that he cannot put the horse's forces into play to a degree sufficient for the use that we would want to make of the horse?

In the chapter in *"Méthode d'équitation"* that follows the *rassembler* and carries the title: "The use of the horse's forces by the rider," the author begins by treating of the canter, and it is an easy task for us to show how this canter of Baucher's is extremely defective for the use that notably a rider of the 2nd class would need to make of it.

This end use that for us, in the *mise en main* and the *relèvement* of the horse as well as in the training at the canter, is the guiding principle that we bring, especially – as it has already been indicated – to the use of the various types of the walk, to prepare the horse for the bounds of the canter; but then to the education of the faculties of the bounding gait that are proper to the canter in such a way that not by the fact of this training, not by the ulterior intensive use of this gait, would it be able to bring prejudice to the various sorts of walk.

One cannot resolve this extremely important problem by the use of the Baucher method; it is only in the old school that one finds the means, and these means come from placing the whole body of the horse into balance, but principally from his correct suppleness and lightness that cannot be obtained other than by this placing into balance.

The suppling of the horse has not been described in detail, especially by the old masters, presumably because they could not imagine that one might understand it in absolutely the wrong way so as to practice it, so to say, locally. But this idea of suppling only certain parts of the horse's body, without corresponding development of the other parts, can only thwart the harmony of the gait and the power of the rider over his horse.

Perfect suppleness and lightness rely on the perfectly balanced position of all parts of the horse's body, and, as soon as the body is in this position, as is the case in the correct *rassembler*, the weight is carried according to need on one or the other hind leg and is found so to say to be concentrated in a pivot. It is evident that the smallest movement of a turn or oscillation will suffice to determine, without effort and in a measure that one could calculate with great exactitude, the line of the direction of the horse's body, because any movement effectuated around a pivot easily displaces the body without changing its form, while, it is true, the supports of the mass, the hind legs, alternate, but the mass properly said is not submitted to change in a visible form.

But if one has, like M. Baucher, sought to obtain suppleness by flexion and supplings practiced on certain parts of the horse without cohesion with the rest of the body, then since the horse does not find himself completely in a position of balance, the rider is obliged, at each moment and changing of the leg supporting the mass of the body, to act on the body of the horse, that is to say on the mass of the body itself; and this continual intervention considerably impedes precision as well as regularity, and therefore the correct rhythm of the movement.

Since M. Baucher does not understand the balanced position of the whole body of the horse, such as we would accomplish it, and he does not prepare his horse starting with the hindquarters but rather with the forehand, he is then obliged to resort to means that, thanks to our lifting of the head and neck and the flexion of the stifle joints, not only do we not need, but that we have to avoid because they alter the vigor that is quite natural to the horse, the movements of the walk and trot, the same as his aptitude to bound in the canter. We have noticed these means that M. Baucher employs, principally to obtain the canter, in the whole method of training that he has followed up to now, notably in the trick that he uses to give his horse this seductive flexibility that he qualifies under the name "suppleness," while he calls "lightness" the floating of the reins that is produced as a result of his manner of *ramener* and the complete absence of normal contact that takes on the appearance of an advantage in the eyes of the profane, when in reality it is one of the greatest vices of the whole method. Into the same category of means we must assign the turns and tight changes of direction that rapidly follow each other at a very collected walk and at a held-back trot. Toward this goal he sometimes makes half turns and figures of eight that are very tight.

In Baucher's changes of direction, the outside leg acts before the inside leg, the rider does not bring his weight to the inside in the turn, and the outside rein is also the first to act; that is why, the more that the turns are frequent and notably tighter, the horse is habituated to shift his weight onto the outside hind leg; and this preparation gives him, in a convenient manner, the inclination to the canter, in which as expected it is the outside hind leg that is the most weighted.

It is thus that, by the turn to the right, M. Baucher gets control over the left hind and prepares the horse for the canter to the right.

If M. Baucher has little use for the correct position for the trot or the "*pli*" position that is so indispensable to us for obtaining a good trot, he has no more of a need for a particular position for the canter. What is more: his trained horse does not even know the flexions that the position of the canter requires for us: the bending in the ribs, so important, and the lateral placement of the head that turns along the line from the poll to the back of the jaw.

In the canter on one track, the body of his horse is placed *completely straight*; in the work on two tracks at the canter as at other gaits, the croup passes the shoulders, and the horse's position is then oblique, without lateral flexion. If he rides his horse with the head placed to the right or to the left, this position is obtained by the flexion of the neck, while with us the neck must necessarily be maintained straight.

Now if in his canter Monsieur Baucher wants to make his outside leg act first, he exposes himself to the horse escaping him to the inside with his croup, to consequently having him get out of the straight position that alone allows him to canter in his manner. Yet since he does not put the horse to the canter by a preliminary action of the outside leg, for example, of the left leg to canter to the right, he needs to use, as exercises preparatory to the canter, in addition to the turns mentioned above, the counter changes of direction, because by the counter changes of direction to the left, for example, he habituates the horse to sufficiently set the left hind under the action of tractions on the reins toward the left.

Once M. Baucher considers that his horse, by these turns, is sufficiently prepared for the exercises at the canter, he collects the horse and sends him forward, straight in the shoulders and the haunches, at a very retained walk, then reinforcing the effect of the reins by twisting the hand more strongly in the wrist and he carries it, to canter for example to the right, against the left side; at the same time, he leans his body to the same side – however, in a fashion hardly perceptible, because of his seat on the fork – but more toward the foreleg than the hind leg. In this fashion, M. Baucher, by the action of the reins, holds in their forward movement the two legs on the left side; but, furthermore, in a special way, by the shifting of his weight, he weights the left fore and this aid is quite remarkable in the execution of his changes of lead.

So therefore he has placed the horse in the position for the depart at the canter, to the right, or, as he says, he has positioned the horse for the movement. Now he collects the horse in this position and from that, fixes the left hind leg for a moment; then he gives, by means of his right leg, the impulsion for the movement forward which, the outside legs of the horse being weighted, becomes the canter, and immediately afterward, he releases the reins, which liberates the weak spring force that, given his manner of placing the horse, can be developed in the hock and produces a hopping movement almost analogous to the gallop of a jackrabbit.

M. Baucher, in making the legs act before the hands, disrupts the natural order of the raising and posing of the horse's legs, and it is precisely as a consequence of this disruption that an imperfect movement is produced.

We know that the horse, in the canter to the right, for example, lifts, at the first beat, the right fore, at the second beat, the left fore and the right hind simultaneously, and at the third beat, the left hind. (We want to speak here of the normal three beat canter that should be the only one that interests us and that most horses are capable of, not only at the beginning of the 3rd stage of higher level dressage, when it has been judiciously prepared, but also when they can move with all of their natural liberty.) But, in M. Baucher's canter to the right, the left fore and the right hind do not rise simultaneously at the second beat; the foreleg rises a little later.

We know, on the other hand, that the feet always regain contact with the ground following exactly the same rhythm, but in the reverse order. That is why, in the correct canter to the right, the left hind, the last lifted, hits the ground first, and the right fore, the first lifted, hits the ground last; the middle beat consists of the two members of the left diagonal that hit the ground simultaneously.

In contrast, when M. Baucher canters to the right, the incorrect lifting of the feet as mentioned above makes the two members of the diagonal not hit the ground simultaneously; the left fore comes to the support of the forehand before the right hind supports the hindquarters; the two beats, however, happen so rapidly that their separation, in particular if the horse is ridden on soft ground, is nearly imperceptible to the ear.

Many of my readers may consider the faults that I have raised and criticized in the canter work of M. Baucher's horses do not present any particularly grave drawback. But if one would imagine, for example, in the canter to the right, the left foreleg hits the ground with such a minimal advance as applies in particular to horses that are heavy in the forehand or to riders of great weight that is then imposed on the foreleg that has returned to the ground too soon.

If we do not want to reduce the utility of the horse by the canter, we must not change the natural play of the legs at this gait in the manner so detrimental as M. Baucher does it. An amelioration of this movement to the profit of the gait and the preparation of the horse could be appropriate only if, for example, in the canter to the right, the rider makes the left foreleg lift a little sooner than the right in such a way that, at the return to the ground, at the second beat, the right hind comes to the support of the mass of the hindquarters sooner than the left fore can support the mass of the forehand. In this fashion, the gait somewhat approaches the four beat school canter and the tendency to irregularities is corrected. We will come back later to the importance of this approach to the school gaits.

In M. Baucher's horses at the canter, one senses an irregular movement of a very unusual character.

It is that of the second beat, the foreleg of the diagonal pair hits the ground before the (inside) hind. That fore leg takes away from the other (outside) hind that is already on the ground part of the weight that that hind leg carries and consequently frees it too much for it to be able afterward to lift and project the body forward by the spring of the hock. Moreover, this outside hind, through the hip and pastern joints, can only exercise its push enough that the movement, instead of being composed of bounds, has something of the walking gaits to it. The old French Masters called this, *"trainer le derrière,"* (behind the trainer) in opposition to the correct way: *"chasser le devant"* (to chase the front.)

Given that in the movement of the hopping canter of a Baucher horse, one would be moved about in the saddle as little as if one cantered a horse that had been trained according to our method and educated by the flexion of the haunches; the reason is that, in the Baucher canter, the shock of the hindquarters, at the moment when it begins to act against the forehand, is already neutralized by the forehand being prematurely returned to the ground.

The surcharge of weight imposed on the forehand in his canter is manifested in the most striking manner at the moment of the *parades* used for halting from the canter or gallop. If the horse is set up at the canter, he does not leave his hind legs in place, even though the reins are released and the legs remain in action – the best proof that the hindquarters escape the control of the rider.

In view of the changes of lead at the canter, as for the canter itself, the tight turns, for Monsieur Baucher, are the principal means of preparation. In the change of direction to the right, for example, he turns his horse at so precipitated a walk that the horse, so as not to fall or to not to have his feet hit one another, takes up the canter to the right for several strides, and he does so all the more easily if, after a half finished change of direction, he is activated by the right leg or the right spur. If a change of direction to the left intervenes here, the reverse aids cause the canter to the left. The more the turns are tightened and brought closer together, the more the horse quickly and voluntarily change the leads, and it is thus that M. Baucher, finally, comes to be able to change the lead at every stride.

This change of lead "tac au tac" (literally tit for tat, refers to every stride, or a-tempo) is a version of the amble, in the genre of a giraffe that we would not hold to be dignified for being mentioned anymore, if they had not made so much noise about the subject, and if even a Chief Rider from the Royal Instruction Squadron, Herr Seidler, had not seriously, in his "Impartial Point of View on the Baucher System," of which he is an adversary, posed this movement, which he found to be difficult for the rider and the horse, as a problem to be resolved for riders and school horses – a proposition that we have not been able to prevent ourselves from considering to be a nice pleasantry. This "difficult problem" is very easy to resolve for someone who knows how to explain it. The explanation is the following:

We have mentioned above how, in the Baucher canter, at the second beat of the hooves' hitting the ground, for example, in the canter to the right, the left fore touches the ground sooner than the diagonal right hind; from there, it becomes possible for Monsieur Baucher to act with his leg on this hind leg while still off the ground, causing it to hit the ground more to the left, therefore more to the side under the body, so well that the left hind finds itself free and the right hind, from the next bound, now becomes the controlling leg and consequently this bound is already a canter to the left. Moreover, with this result another factor cooperates: that factor is the movement of the rider that alternatively weighs on one or the other foreleg by leaning the upper body forward and toward the side to be held back.

After this explanation, the reader who reflects will see clearly that all the faults that one must reproach in the Baucher canter must, in addition to his other faults, be attributed to the fact that he has refused to give the horse liberty of the shoulders by the raising of the head and neck and perfect flexion of the haunches by the bending of the stifle joints. If he acts with the forehand to the rear, the effect finds itself produced directly against the hock and pastern, which impedes the coiling of the spring, frees the hind legs too much, and on the contrary surcharges the forelegs.

M. Baucher seduces the onlooker with his canter by the facility with which the horse gets used to it; and for the riders that find that easy and that do not attach much importance to the fact that, by such exercises, this canter will prejudice impulsion, especially at the trot, for these riders, the procedure could certainly keep its worth; they require too little of the horse, and if the horse gives them this little, they can well content themselves with it.

Among the exercises in use for the training of the ridden horse, M. Baucher, to finish, goes on to mention in his "*Méthode d'équitation,*" the *piaffe.*

The true piaffe can only be obtained from the school trot. M. Baucher does not know this trot and realizes his piaffe from the exercises of the downward flexion, of the attacks, and of concentration. Without a doubt, the movement that he consequently obtains can be taught to each horse in little time, as M. Baucher undertakes with complacency.

If in effect, the horse, even otherwise insensitive to any external impression, is held for a certain period of time between the hand and the leg like a vise, and if he is then tortured, in one way by successive rapid pokes of the spur on the flanks, always in the same place, and in another way by whacks of the whip, the animal, from impatience or wrath, in order to free himself, develops some energy by stamping in place. If after several gestures of this kind, he is delivered from this torment, he soon responds with submission to the demand of the rider, from fear of feeling it start again.

One must say that M. Baucher is extremely modest in his requirements. When his horse, over the course of these exercises, stamps his forelegs anxiously, beats the ground, and, so to say, kneads it, given that he raises and lowers these same members without much enthusiasm, for such irregularities Baucher goes as far as caressing him instead of punishing him. As to the hind legs, they have too high an action, a sort of *"mouvement de harper"* (La Guérinière qualified it in a very characteristic fashion as *"dégingandé"*(lanky, ungainly, gangling)), as a result of which the croup stays at its natural height, but the forelegs, while lifting, stay too close to the ground. Furthermore, the hind legs escape to the side and cause a shifting of the horse's body from right to left and left to right.

These oscillations cannot be produced in a correct piaffe, but are very explainable in the case of M. Baucher by reason of the bad placer and the defective *rassembler* that is the result.

If M. Baucher, besides the direct propulsive aids, also had our indirect propulsive aids, he could give his horse another placer and from that a better *rassembler*. In the piaffe, the horse must be collected in a manner such that the centre of gravity falls exactly at the point where the diagonals cross. Then the force carrying the haunches is made to contribute exactly in the same way as that of the shoulders, and the hind legs consequently do not develop any pushing force that could throw weight to the front and to the side. With M. Baucher, on the contrary, the centre of gravity is too far in front so the force carrying the shoulders makes more of a contribution than the haunches; the haunches are therefore free and their pushing force is used to alternatively throw the centre of gravity from one side to the other on the forward diagonal; but at the same time, the hind legs, precisely because of their too great a liberty, escape to the side or backward, instead of always returning to their tracks.

M. Baucher mentions that it is possible for him, following the more or less rapid alternation of the lateral aids, to make the horses piaffe more quickly or more slowly, and by that he shows his total incomprehension of the exercise. The piaffe is a school air and cannot therefore, when it is perfected, have but one cadence.

As for us, we have no special need to work at the piaffe, because this movement results naturally from our preparatory exercises, notably the school trot, and because we use it only for a few strides as a means to come to a perfect *rassembler*, but without making it a lesson properly said.

To exercise at the piaffe horses who are not trained for the goal of savant equitation aiming for perfection, is not only useless, but even disadvantageous; because experience shows that a horse so trained, when he is supposed to remain at rest, often wants to put himself into movement against the wishes of his rider and he manifests his intention by stamping his feet.

We have now come to the conclusion of what we have had to say in detail about M. Baucher and his method, and we have shown again, in a general way, what is the source of the defects in his method, what are the essential traits that are found in all of his exercises: beside these exercises, we must place, in order to make a comparison, our method that, from the beginning, proposes and does the contrary to what M. Baucher presents as correct.

Our principle is: *strengthen the horse in movement for the movement*. On the contrary, M. Baucher's work tends to weaken the propulsive forces to be able to dominate the horse more easily.

He pretends to have as much more power over the horse as the horse has a greater number of feet on the ground; us, as much more power as the horse has feet in the air.

M. Baucher knows very well where the source of the forces of resistance is; in the hindquarters; however he seeks to conquer them at the point where they are found, in the forehand. Us, on the contrary, we know that the forces of resistance are none other than those that, at the same time, favor the movement; that is why we seek to concentrate the forces more in their source, the hindquarters, so that they change the line of their action to the direction where, instead of confounding our intentions, they are put to our service.

M. Baucher weights that part of the horse's body that, at rest, is the weakest of the two and by reason of his structure, has the least elasticity, *the forehand. Us, we weight* the strongest, *the hind-*

quarters and from its elastic structure, we favor the progressive forces that lie in there.

If the horse stays in the position that he takes in free movement, we seek to neutralize the *weight of the rider*, of which the action can only be paralyzing, by artificially placing the upper parts of the forehand to the rear. *M. Baucher makes his horse feel the weight of the rider yet more* by making these upper parts of the forehand weigh to the front more than is the case when the horse is in a state of liberty.

He keeps *the same position of the horse* from the start to the end of his work. But us, over the course of training, we have need for *two different preparatory positions*, for getting to the normal position, our ideal.

In the same way, M. Baucher's *position* remains *constantly unchanged*, while, us, *we change it*, adapting it, partly to the movements, partly to the stages of training.

M. Baucher, in his work, begins by *the forehand* while, us, we attack *the hindquarters*, by means of which we make ourselves masters of the forehand.

By actions that are constantly the same and nearly uninterrupted work *with ineffective spurs, he blunts the horse's sensitivity to the legs* and from this fact is constrained afterward to constantly intervene with the spur, while *by the progressive intensity of effects and the use of sharp spurs*, we augment the horse's respect for the legs, and then have no more need for their continued action.

By this ensemble of procedures, M. Baucher blocks the impulsion in the horse, taking rapidity away from him, and he cannot make the horse develop any energy in the movement. At the same time, the rider is, from this fact, constrained to remedy with meticulous care the irregularities of the hindquarters, which he must constantly push forward and prevent from escaping to the side. The walk becomes creeping and the canter becomes hopping.

If one adds that his corrections generally consist of making flexions in place, or of walk to the side or backwards, of executing turns and changes of direction, and that consequently, if resistances come up, it is impossible for him to reduce them in forward movement, one can then see that his horses can only be suitable to a completely secondary order of use.

But as soon as one makes serious efforts to make demands on these horses, as for example, for the hunt or for cavalry service, they can only show themselves unusable, and furthermore, they are found to be ruined sooner than the horses that respond to such requirements; because it is a known fact that movements that are energetic and regular, conserve, while movements that are sloppy and incorrect, ruin.

Consequently, there is nothing astonishing in that M. Baucher, despite the great favor that he enjoyed with high French military figures of the time, has seen his method abandoned after a short period of practice in his country's cavalry; nothing astonishing in that the trials that he has done here in Berlin, in the dressage of many horses at the Royal Academy of Equitation have given results unfavorable to him and to the introduction of his method.

BIBLIOGRAPHY

Faverot de Kerbrech, General - *Methodical Dressage of the Riding Horse and Dressage of the Outdoor Horse,* Xenophon Press, Franktown VA, 2010

Fillis, James – *Principles of Dressage and Equitation,* Xenophon Press, Franktown VA, 2017

L'Hotte, General – *Un Officier de Cavalerie,* Hazan, Paris, 1958

Licart, Commandant – *Évolutions Équestres, à travers les ages,* Olivier Perrin Éditeur, Paris, 1963

Nelson, Hilda – *François Baucher, The Man and his Method,* Xenophon Press, Franktown VA, 2013

Alexis-François L'Hotte, *The Quest for Lightness in Equitation,* J. A. Allen, London, 1997

CREDITS

We wish to thank for their help:
The Documentation Service of the National School of Equitation
as well as
The Library of the Armour and Cavalry School
and
The Library of the Château de Saumur

XENOPHON PRESS LIBRARY
www.XenophonPress.com

Xenophon Press is dedicated to the preservation of classical equestrian literature. We bring both new and old works to English-speaking riders.

30 Years with Master Nuno Oliveira, Henriquet 2011

A New Method to Dress Horses, Cavendish 2017

A Rider's Survival from Tyranny, de Kunffy 2012

Another Horsemanship, Racinet 1994

Austrian Art of Riding, Poscharnigg 2015

Baucher and His School, Decarpentry 2011

Classic Show Jumping: the de Nemethy Method, de Nemethy 2016

Divide and Conquer Book 1, Lemaire de Ruffieu 2016

Divide and Conquer Book 2, Lemaire de Ruffieu 2017

Dressage for the 21st Century, Belasik 2001

Dressage in the French Tradition, Diogo de Bragança 2011

Dressage Principles and Techniques, Tavora 2017

Dressage Principles Illuminated, Expanded Edition, de Kunffy 2017

École de Cavalerie Part II, Robichon de la Guérinière 1992, 2015

Equine Osteopathy: What the Horses Have Told Me, Giniaux 2014

Fragments from the writings of Max Ritter von Weyrother, Fane 2017

François Baucher: The Man and His Method, Baucher/Nelson 2013

Great Horsewomen of the 19th Century in the Circus, Nelson 2015

Gymnastic Exercises for Horses Volume II, Eleanor Russell 2013

H. Dv. 12 Cavalry Manual of Horsemanship, Reinhold 2014

Handbook of Jumping Essentials, Lemaire de Ruffieu 2015

Handbook of Riding Essentials, Lemaire de Ruffieu 2015

Healing Hands, Giniaux, DVM 1998

Horse Training: Outdoors and High School, Beudant 2014

I, Siglavy, Asay 2018

Learning to Ride, Santini 2016

Legacy of Master Nuno Oliveira, Millham 2013

Lessons in Lightness, Mark Russell 2016

Methodical Dressage of the Riding Horse, Faverot de Kerbrech 2010

Principles of Dressage and Equitation, a.k.a. Breaking and Riding, Fillis 2017

Racinet Explains Baucher, Racinet 1997

Science and Art of Riding in Lightness, Stodulka 2015

The Art of Riding a Horse or Description of Modern Manége in Its Perfection, D'Eisenberg 2015

The Art of Traditional Dressage, Volume I DVD, de Kunffy 2013

The Ethics and Passions of Dressage Expanded Ed., de Kunffy 2013

The Forward Impulse, Santini 2016

The Gymnasium of the Horse, Steinbrecht 2017

The Horses, a novel, Elaine Walker 2015

The Italian Tradition of Equestrian Art, Tomassini 2014

The Maneige Royal, de Pluvinel 2010, 2015

The Portuguese School of Equestrian Art, de Oliveira/da Costa 2012

The Spanish Riding School & Piaffe and Passage, Decarpentry 2013

To Amaze the People with Pleasure and Delight, Walker 2015

Total Horsemanship, Racinet 1999

Training with Master Nuno Oliveira double DVD set, Eleanor Russell 2016

Truth in the Teaching of Master Nuno Oliveira, Eleanor Russell 2015

Wisdom of Master Nuno Oliveira, de Coux 2012

Available at www.XenophonPress.com

www.ingramcontent.com/pod-product-compliance
Lightning Source LLC
Chambersburg PA
CBHW050631300426
44112CB00012B/1754